UNREMEMBERED 2

UNREME

MBERED

BOOK 2: ACTORS, ARTISTS, ENTERTAINERS & INFLUENCERS

KEN ZURSKI

AUTHOR OF *PEORIA STORIES* &
THE WRECK OF THE COLUMBIA

Unremembered Book 2: Actors, Artists, Entertainers & Influencers
© Copyright 2022, Ken Zurski

First Edition   ISBN 13: 978-1-956872-11-8

AMIKA PRESS   466 Central AVE #23 Northfield IL 60093   847 920 8084
info@amikapress.com   Available for purchase on amikapress.com

Edited by Mark Henry Larson and Ann Wambach.

Cover design by Sarah Koz. Photographs left to right: James Barrie, The Library of Congress, part of the Bain Collection [1908–1915]; Sada Yacco, see page 41; Felix Nadar, self-portrait, The Bibliothèque nationale de France, part of the Gallica Digital Library, public domain; Edward Steichen, see page 13; Maude Adams, Otto Sarony Co., public domain [1901]; Isadora Duncan, The Library of Congress, part of the Bain Collection. Background photograph by jmnb56, freeimages.com.

Title page photograph: Rita Jolivet at a War Bond rally in New York City, The Library of Congress, part of the Bain Collection [1918].

Author photograph by Nora Zurski. Index by Stephen Seddon. Designed & typeset by Sarah Koz. Set in Walbaum, designed by Walbaum Justus Erich in 1800, digitized by František Štorm in 2010. Thanks to Nathan Matteson.

DEDICATED TO THOSE WHO DEVOTE THEIR LIVES
TO THE ARTS AND THE ENTERTAINMENT OF OTHERS

This book is about the entertainment industry as a whole around the time *Peter Pan* first appeared, not the history of *Peter Pan* itself. Most people know the story and character of Peter Pan solely through the 1953 animated Walt Disney feature based mostly on a popular musical version of the play. But when *Peter Pan* debuted on stage in the early years of the twentieth century, it was all new. Audiences were seeing it for the first time with no preconceived notions. *Peter Pan, or the Boy Who Wouldn't Grow Up* was whimsical and heartwarming, for sure, but also tragic and sad in parts. And while the story was about children, it was not specifically intended just for children. Unfortunately, these days this original production is rarely seen; what's left to the ages is mostly the musical version and Disney's movie. But many people were impacted by its success both directly and indirectly. Their stories, although broader in scope, are in some respects forever linked to either the play itself or by associations to those who were involved with the play's origins.

To present this story, I have limited my resources mostly to firsthand accounts such as autobiographies, diaries, or letters. Secondhand accounts such as biographies by other authors fill in the rest. To reduce the amount of back notes, whenever possible credits for books, newspapers, or other periodicals are listed within the text. Some quotes, written or spoken, have been altered slightly for clarity without changing the substance of the thought. Oftentimes, where recorded history ends, speculation begins. Any opinions or speculation by other authors is duly noted.

Contents

Contents

PETER PAN..Miss MAUDE ADAMS
MR. DARLING...ERNEST LAWFORD
MRS. DARLING...GRACE HENDERSON
WENDY MOIRA ANGELA DARLING...............MILDRED MORRIS
JOHN NAPOLEON DARLING.....................WALTER ROBINSON
MICHAEL NICOLAS DARLING....................MARTHA McGRAW
NANA..CHARLES H. WESTON
TINKER BELL...JANE WREN
TOOTLES............⎫   ⎧..........VIOLET RAND
NIBS.....................⎪   ⎪.........LULU PECK
SLIGHTLY.............⎪   ⎪...PRANCES SEDGWICK
CURLY.................⎬ Members of Peter's Band. ⎨.........MABEL KIPP
FIRST TWIN.........⎪   ⎪KATHERINE KAPPELL
SECOND TWIN.....⎭   ⎩.........ELLA GILROY
JAMES HOOK, the pirate captain.....................ERNEST LAWFORD
SMEE...................⎫   ⎧.............THOMAS McGRATH
STARKEY..........⎬ Pirates. ⎨.........WALLACE JACKSON

"Interior of the Empire Theatre, New York". The Miriam and Ira D. Wallach Division of Art, Prints and Photographs: Photography Collection, *The New York Public Library Digital Collections* [1860-1920].

UNREMEMBERED 2

Mrs. Pat Campbell as Eliza Doolitle in *Pygmalion*. The Library of Congress, part of the Bain Collection [1913-1915].

Act I

⁓ "Nothing in Nature is more certain than the fact that no single thing or event can stand alone. It is attached to all that has gone before it, and it will remain attached to all that will follow it. It was born of some cause, and so it must be followed by some effect in an endless chain." –*Julian P. Johnson*

Mrs. Patrick Campbell listened intently to every word. She closed her eyes at times, mesmerized by the charming Irish lilt of the man reading a play to her. The more he expressed each line, the more entranced she became.

The man was George Bernard Shaw and the play he was reading was his own. He had asked the popular London actress known to everyone as Mrs. Pat to hear it. The two knew each other. Recently, they had been exchanging letters and she had teasingly told him she did not care much for his work. Now he was in her drawing room.

"That's not a nice sound, Mr. Shaw," she interrupted after he read one of the lines. He repeated it again, a deep cockney drawl that hardly sounded like English at all.

"Ah-ah-ah-ow-oo" is how she had heard it.

Just days before, Shaw had been told by George Alexander, Mrs. Pat's manager, that portraying Eliza Doolittle, the young flower girl in Shaw's new play *Pygmalion,* might be a stretch for Mrs. Pat. For one thing, she was too old.

Shaw had no such reservations. In fact, he had expressively written the play for Mrs. Pat. Shaw believed only a veteran actress could pull off the critical balance needed in scenes with a domineering male lead, in this case a linguistics professor attempting to teach a Cockney flower girl how to be a proper, high society lady.

Alexander was adamant. He graciously offered to pay another actress of Shaw's choosing to take the lead instead. Shaw rejected his notion and went directly to Mrs. Pat. "Ah-ah-ah-ow-oo," Shaw said again, just so she had heard the line correctly.

She repeated the line and asked: "You don't think I'm too ripe to play this role at forty-five, do you Mr. Shaw?"

He corrected her. "You mean at fifty?"

Mrs. Pat smiled sheepishly.

Shaw knew he had his Eliza.

1

More picturesque than fatal

⚲ Part of the charms afforded to those who attended the 1867 Paris World's Fair, known as the second L'Exposition Universelle, was not just the many wonders they could behold on the ground, but the sights they experienced when they looked up as well. While most buildings, including the circular-shaped and nearly mile-long-in circumference Main Hall, were no more than a few stories tall, the English Lighthouse, for example, stood at nearly fifty meters in height and boasted an open, steel grid-work design that one unimpressed French writer described as an eyesore that "dishonors the Champ de Mars with its fleshy skeleton."

Opinion aside, the lighthouse, with its sloping base and cupola top, was a pattern by which architect Gustave Eiffel would give the city its symbolic footprint years later with a massive wrought-iron tower that stood three hundred meters in height and was large enough to support a hydraulic lift that brought tourists up and down from the top without a single step. This "elevator," as it was called, was just one invention among many that were showcased at the fair.

But for those lucky enough to be at the fair when the wind was blowing just right, looking upward might mean seeing a large balloon soaring overhead, casting a long moving shadow on the proceedings below. "[The balloon] which I declare beforehand, without fear of contradiction, shall be the most beautiful spectacle which has ever been given to mankind to speculate," is how it was promoted by its creator, Gaspard-Félix Tournachon, the premier French balloonist of his time. Better known as Félix Nadar, or Nadar for short, a name he self-appointed after one of his inventions called "Nadar" just looked good as a billboard promoting himself.

Born in 1820, Nadar's early adult life as a printmaker in turn morphed into a career as a commercial artist. His widely exaggerated illustrations of popular artists, writers, actors, and musicians of the day appeared in many of Paris's journals, magazines, and newspapers. However once he concocted the idea to combine his caricatures into a mosaic piece, print them on one sheet, and sell them as posters, the result became so popular that Nadar the brand became synonymous with his work.

Then he found photography.

"Photography is a marvelous discovery," he wrote in imitable fashion, "a science that engages the most elevated intellects, an art that sharpens the wits of the wisest souls—and the practical application of which lies within capacity of the shallowest imbecile."

Though Nadar wanted to make pictures he could sell, he also hoped to find better and more efficient ways to take them. He began to experiment and soon patented several new inventions including an automatic "sliding lens shutter," which sped up the exposure time. Nadar opened a photography studio in Paris and instead of penciling drawings of the city's greatest celebrities, this time he began shooting those same stars on film in his studio.

This is where the balloons came in. Until then, landscape pictures could only be taken from ground level or from heights reachable by climbing. What if, Nadar wondered, he could take them from the air as well? There were a few obstacles to this theory that needed to be addressed, not the least of which was how to get a camera as high as the clouds. To Nadar, there was an obvious solution to this conundrum: balloons.

So Nadar became a balloonist.

Bigger and better was always Nadar's way of forging ahead. So he started to envision ballooning itself as a revenue source, not just

Felix Nadar in a balloon gondola. Studio portrait, public domain [1863].

as a means to get better photographs, but also as a means of travel too. A balloon or something close to it could be used as transport, he thought, rather than just an observation post. People and commerce, even the mail, could be moved much quicker by a balloon.

Here Nadar had some basic aeronautic principles already solved: the gas balloon was lighter than air and therefore could rise and stay aloft. But with no human way to control it, how far could it travel? To date, attempts to stretch the limitations of an untethered and manned balloon had been sketchy in both Europe and America. Considering the amount of time it would take before a flying machine, even a dirigible, equipped with a good navigation system and steering was realized, Nadar's thinking was revolutionary.

To try, though, now that was the spirit!

Naming it appropriately *Le Géant,* Nadar unveiled his balloon. It was as much to prove at least that a balloon could carry more than just a few people at a time. Ultimately, and not surprisingly, the controllability issue would be its downfall, but not without Nadar, as befitting his style, launched it to great fanfare on October 4, 1863.

As for the balloon itself, its massive size was one wonder; the other was the basket, now more like a gondola with wickerwork walls that resembled a small house complete with patricians inside and windows for viewing. On top was an open-aired sundeck.

Fifteen intrepid souls went on board that day; all fifteen got back on the ground safely. Initially, Nadar asked that no women or children go on the flight, but at the last minute he succumbed to the charms of a young aristocratic lady and granted her wish to come along. Each patron paid a thousand francs for the privilege. While the inaugural flight was five hours long, shorter than planned, an encouraged Nadar quickly readied another lift, a long-distance venture he advertised, which would take place two weeks later.

That one didn't go so well.

Despite a good start, on that day the farther the balloon traveled the worse it got. The wind changed direction and became stronger. Nadar lowered *Le Géant* closer to the ground, but the balloon did not slow down. He instructed the passengers to brace for an emergency landing, a maneuver with which even he was unfamiliar. The balloon dragged and bounced for nearly a half hour. The terrified passengers grabbed anything they could to hold on. Some even grasped the balloons guide wires like a rope for support, pulling the balloon down even further. Eventually the balloon flew into a thicket of trees, shredded, and slowed in the process. When the gondola finally came to rest, several people had already been thrown off. Everyone had an injury of some kind, including Nadar who fractured both his legs, but surprisingly no one was killed. Nearly eighteen hours after liftoff and four hundred miles from Paris, the balloon was now resting, crumpled and deflated near Nienburg, Germany.

Despite his injuries, Nadar's spirit was still intact. *Four hundred miles!* Now that was something! Even more sensational was a harrowing scrape with an express train. Nadar commissioned an artist to make an illustrated representation of the balloon's close call with the train and placed it in a journal as a companion piece to his book, *Mémoires du Géant,* which featured a thirty-two-page description of the failed journey. It sold well.

After the failed second flight, Nadar took *Le Géant* out for public exhibitions and continued to promote the idea of flight as a means of transportation. No one had to be convinced that balloons, while fast, were likely not the answer, at least not yet. But a winged contraption, perhaps one with a propeller on top, could do the trick. Fundamentally, Nadar's ideas—imagined rather than seen—had some merit. He enlisted some important friends to help. Among them was Victor Hugo who called Nadar a symbol of French patriotism. Thanks to Hugo's endorsement, Nadar became something of a folk hero in his home country. And for those who came to Paris in 1867 to discover the fair's many new innovations, looking up meant seeing Nadar's giant balloon in one grand final flight: "the Vertical Journey," as Hugo put it.

In all, *Le Géant* made three uneventful flights during the fair. The ascents were only for short distances and the balloon flew just fine. Its appearance however was another matter: tattered and worn with strips of sewn-on silk, like bandages covering its "many wounds," as one witness described it. As *Le Géant* passed overhead, observers could hear the steam seeping out, while puffs of smoke like that from a locomotive came from the patched-up rips near the top. It was as sad as it was humorous, but on every flight there was Nadar, smiling and sticking his body halfway out one of the gondola's windows, camera in hand ready to capture another shot of the festivities below.

The fair itself was notable for being the most photographed of any world exhibition up to that point. Advances in technology were the main reasons why, but also a sweeping interest in photography was developing, especially in France. Not only could pictures be sold to the public as stereocards, but painters and sculptors were becoming interested buyers as well. They wanted to create in their own styles the images captured on film. Nadar could claim the originality of taking photos from up above, but on the ground a slew of France's finest photography studios took on the task of recording the fair's many exhibits for prosperity.

Among them was Léon & Lévy, a publishing company and editing house that opened in Paris in 1864. The Léon of Léon & Lévy was Moyse Léon, and the Lévy was Georges Lévy, better known as Isaac, Moyse's father-in-law. Together they took many of the pictures preserved from the fair, including those of the statuaries that dotted the grounds. They also captured images of other nations' exhibits and people, such as the Tunisian and Mongolian representatives posing in cultural costumes.

Not much else is known about the firm until later in 1895 when Lévy's two sons Abraham and Gaspard took over the business and became Lévy Fils et Cie (Lévy Sons) or LL for short. Perhaps inspired by the interest in the fair, Lévy Fils et Cie found a way to break into the postcard business, at that time popular in France. They produced hundreds of landscape photos from Europe, Asia, Africa, and even America, all under the LL banner. Their foray into postcards also included a number of seriates, entitled "Oriental Postcards." The title alone does not quite explain what these entailed. True, the cards were oriental in nature, depicting women from mostly Asian countries, even Arabic women from western Asia. But unlike the pictures from the fair of cultured woman in full traditional regale, these women were shot in a studio and seen mostly topless.

This was not a new concept, especially in Paris, where painters and sculptors had been depicting nudes for years. For the Lévys, though, the realism of the photos was raw and unflinching, and the business of nudes on film soon became a very lucrative trade. Even Félix Nadar dabbled in nude pictures before his aerial adventures began. A series of these sensuous photos show women unclothed and tagged with only their professional names, *Mimi* or *Mariette (standing nude)* and the like.

After the fair in 1867, while Nadar's aerial photos gained popularity, *Le Géant* was never seen again. The balloon was dragged from the grounds and tucked away forever. The wicker gondola, one observer stated, was now better suited for "matchwood."

Nadar never achieved the kind of success he aspired to with the balloons, but his portraits of France's finest statesmen, artists, and literary figures are considered signature works. As for aviation in general, Nadar was just one month short of his ninetieth birthday when two American brothers from Dayton, Ohio, Wilber and Orville Wright, brought their flying machine to France in 1908 for an exhibition, showing once and for all that man could achieve sustained flight—something Nadar had envisioned all along.

Nadar died two years later.

For the Lévy Sons, their lasting significance would come unexpectedly in one distinctive photo taken on October 22, 1895, a Tuesday, and a rather uneventful start to another early weekday in France. On that day, a passenger rail express was traveling from the seaside village of Granville to Montparnasse, a quaint neighborhood in the southeast section of Paris. A normal nonstop seven hour and ten minute trip, the train was running late. A young railroad man at the tender age of nineteen, engineer Guillame Marie Pellerin, tried to make up the time by picking up speed and intending to slow down only as they approached the station. In theory it should have worked. The train was equipped with a Westinghouse air brake that would considerably slow down the train from cruising speed when the locomotives brakes could not. This time, however, when Pellerin activated the air brake, it failed. He reached for the hand brake, but it was too late. The train barreled into the sta-

"Train Wreck at Montparnasse Station". Levy & Fils (Sons), photographer, public domain [1895].

tion, through the buffer, across the concourse, and right through the station's brick wall, sending the locomotive nose-first thirty feet down to Place de Rennes below. The coal car, still attached, was dangling as well, and the first car behind it was barely sticking out of the wall. The rest of the cars were in the station, intact with most remaining on the tracks. No one on the train—not the passengers, not even the poor engineer who jumped and escaped with only minor bruises—was seriously hurt. "More picturesque than fatal" the *Pall Mall Gazette* announced the next day.

But as details came forth, an unsuspecting victim emerged, a woman named Marie-Augustine Aguilard, a newspaper vendor's wife who just happened to be in front of the station when the train barreled through the wall. Her husband had gone to retrieve the evening papers and left Maria in charge. Although the train's locomotive missed her on the way down, a masonry brick the size of large box struck her on the head, presumably killing her instantly. Her body was discovered in the debris below.

The locomotive sat in its immobile, downward state for days, so photographers were able to get several shots from various angles. The most famous one is attributed to the studio of Lévy Sons. It is taken from ground level and shows the full locomotive from the left side off the front. Trains wrecked in many different and unusual ways, but this was quite skewed in both its composition and staging.

Indeed, the power of the photograph was just beginning when the Lévy brothers, previously unknown except for collectors of the French landscape and "Oriental Cards," put their stamp on history. Dramatic images like the Montparnasse train-wreck photo and others like it would soon spur on budding young artists who had now found a new medium ready to explore and exploit.

One of them was a man named Edward Steichen.

2

Craft is only a means

ᘒ In 1901 Edward Steichen came to Paris from America. Like many other young artists, he brought along a portfolio filled with paintings and photographs. He also had the backing of perhaps the most-talked-about photographer at the time, Alfred Stieglitz.

Born in Hoboken, New Jersey, in 1864 to wealthy German immigrants, Stieglitz studied mechanical engineering and chemistry in Berlin. He discovered photography in a course based on the practical science of the process. It would help him be a better mechanical engineer he was told, something his domineering father had wanted for his son all along. Stieglitz studied the science of photo making, specifically the work being done on color-sensitive plates. He bought a small box camera with a single lens and took to the streets.

Until then, the popular camera clubs that popped up mainly in Europe were dismissed as mere hobby clubs. Stieglitz had other ideas. He opened the Camera Club of New York and became editor of *Camera Notes,* a journal showcasing the so-called "artistic" photographs, using light and shadow to create beautiful streetscapes and landscapes that were pleasingly satisfying—not just showing a place for its own sake, but capturing its mood as well. With this attitude, came controversy. Stieglitz embraced it. He purposely called on "amateur" photographers to produce more "artistic"

Edward Steichen, self-portrait. *Vanity Fair,* public domain [1923].

Alfred Stieglitz. The Library of Congress, Gertrude Kaeseber, photographer [1902].

work and shamed those who didn't. Painting clubs mostly snubbed him. All this made Stieglitz even more determined. "I have all but killed myself for photography," he once declared later in his life.

In the spring of 1900, Edward Steichen stepped into Stieglitz's Camera Club as a fresh and eager twenty-one-year-old from the Midwest. It was a monumental meeting for both men. In Steichen, Stieglitz had found just what he was looking for, a gifted young painter and photographer who could advance his principles of both applications in pictorial photography. "I think I found my man," he told his wife about Steichen. In return, Steichen would say that he never "planned for the future" without Stieglitz's advice.

Just days before their meeting, Steichen had kissed his mother goodbye at the family's home in Milwaukee, Wisconsin, and set out east to board a ship. Like many artists his age he was bound for Paris, the art center of the world, to become famous. First he stopped in New York, though, where Steichen met William Merritt Chase, the prominent American painter of his day. Chase encouraged Steichen to follow through with his plans. Then armed with his portfolio, Steichen went to see Stieglitz.

Born in Luxemburg in 1879, Steichen was just a baby when his parents left their homeland to find a better life in America. The Steichens arrived in New York and traveled by train to Chicago. Eventually they settled in Hancock, Michigan, where Jean-Pierre, Edward's father, a farmer back home, could find work in the copper mines—a job for which he was poorly suited. His mother, Marie, found a job in a merchandise store. They worked hard, made little money, and soon found themselves with another mouth to feed, a baby girl named Lilian. Marie was determined that her two children get a good education, so when he was nine she put Edward on a train bound for Milwaukee with a note addressed to a priest they knew, to place him in a local Catholic school. Being competitive and resistant to study, young Edward was not an ideal student at first. However, he was smart and soon grew into the school's strict routines.

Then one day in art class he drew a tulip.

Shortly thereafter Marie received word that her son was a gifted artist. She was advised that they should all move to Milwaukee to be closer to Edward. The next year, they did. As a teenager, Edward quit school and took an apprenticeship with a lithographer. He taught himself the basics of drawing and painting and began to experiment with a new medium, photography.

The study was not effortless. "Photography is a medium of formidable contradictions," he once wrote. "It is both ridiculously easy and almost impossibly difficult."

Steichen's interest in photography was influenced by the 1893 World Columbian Exposition in Chicago, when as a teenager he saved up enough money to purchase a train ticket from Milwaukee to view for himself such new inventions as electricity.

Among the many exhibits on display was the "The Largest Photo in the World," a mosaic comprised of nineteen different photos on a printed sheet, two feet high by fifteen feet wide. Edward was interested in machines and bought a small electric motor at the fair, but the photographs he had seen somehow stuck with him. Two years later at the age of fifteen, on a whim, Steichen walked into a Milwaukee camera shop and began to ask questions. The next year he bought a camera of his own.

Steichen went to Paris as planned, this time with the support of Stieglitz who used his influence to promote the young protégé. Steichen's time in Paris was productive. He entered photographs in prestigious exhibitions and continued to work, including landing a paid commission from the Norwegian landscape-painter Fritz Thaulow, who asked Steichen to take pictures of his two children. At some point during their conversations, they discussed an old friend of Thaulow's, the renowned sculptor Auguste Rodin, who had recently bought property near Thaulow's estate. They should meet, Thaulow insisted. He would introduce them that afternoon.

Steichen was not unfamiliar. As was the case with photography, it is likely the visit to the Chicago World's Fair in 1893 also introduced him to Rodin's work as well. Inside the French Pavilion was an exhibit hidden to the public by drapery and only viewed by request or invitation. Behind the curtains were three works by Rodin, all marble nudes including one called *Cupid and Psyche*. Rodin had sent five works to the fair but only two were deemed appropriate enough to show without concealment. The suppression of his work, however, gave it more power and certainly generated more interest. Rodin had sent the pieces in hopes of selling them. An interested buyer was one of the city's wealthiest and most controversial figures, Charles Tyson Yerkes, whose cutthroat deals, backhanded schemes, and shifty stock machinations made him the "Cable Czar," of Chicago, "cable" in this case referring to cable cars. Despite his reputation as a manipulator and crook, Yerkes would help create one of the largest and most efficient cable systems in the world: the downtown elevated line known as the "El" is his creation. In 1893, however, Yerkes was looking to buy art and chose two of Rodin's works including the heretofore concealed *Cupid and Psyche*.

Whether this spurred Steichen to ask Thaulow about Rodin is not known. Certainly, when Thaulow brought it up Steichen was eager to meet him. Excited, Steichen gathered up his portfolio, tucked it under his arm, and, with Thaulow and his wife leading the way on their bicycles, pedaled to Rodin's studio in the French countryside.

"Craft is only a means," Rodin told him. "But the artist who neglects it will never attain his end, which is the interpretation of feelings and ideas."

This fortuitous meeting between Steichen and Rodin would prove to inherently change the life of the young painter and photographer. However, another chance meeting would also be woven into the thread of this narrative.

Like Steichen, Kathleen Bruce, an English sculptor, had self-imported to France to the Montparnasse section of Paris, where artists lived and where several years earlier that picturesque train wreck had taken place. Steichen noticed her sitting across from him while dining at a small café he frequented. She was not French and looked lost– mostly in the book she was reading, the same book she carried with her every day when she came to lunch.

In 1902, Steichen was still gaining his footing as an artist and likely just as broke as Kathleen. They ate at the same cheap restaurant every day, across from one another, occasionally stealing a glance.

Then one day they met.

3

What are you reading, Esmeralda?

ᑲᕈ Kathleen Bruce was born with royalty in her blood, specifically that of the fourteenth-century king of Scotland, Robert the Bruce, whose brother would found her side of the family line. Her mother, Janie, bore eleven children, with Kathleen being the youngest. Shortly after giving birth to Kathleen in 1878, Janie fell ill and went blind. Two years later she was dead from pneumonia brought on by an outset of Bright's disease. Kathleen's father Lloyd Bruce, a canon of York, would soon remarry. But Lloyd was also sickly and could not take care of all the children. Their stepmother held "little interest," according to Kathleen, so most of her siblings were shipped off to their great-uncle William in Edinburgh. When she was seven, Kathleen joined them. A few years later, her father was dead.

Shortly thereafter, her great-uncle died, and Kathleen was sent to a convent, a place where she witnessed other girls embracing such a religious fervor that angels would appear to them in visions. Not so much for Kathleen. At sixteen she left.

Her family hoped she would choose to be a teacher, but she chose art instead. "Off and away. Let's go to Paris and be artists!" she explained cavalierly.

Without much money, Kathleen struggled to find places to eat, but one suited her well. It was quaint and inexpensive. "I always

Kathleen Bruce. From *A Great Task of Happiness: The Life of Kathleen Scott* by Louisa Young. Public domain.

had my meals at the same restaurant," she later wrote about her time in Montparnasse. "I took a book. I always sat at the same table." One day she noticed a man sitting at another table directly across from her. She had seen him before. He was handsome: exotic with "dark, wavy hair." He looked American and he looked serious, as artists often did when they were sitting alone. "He also brought a book," she charmingly noticed.

Together they sat apart, stealing glances, but nothing more. "Day after day, lunch after lunch," she wrote, "we sat opposite each other, scarcely ever looking up save to catch each other's eye and look down again." Then one day he was gone. Two days passed. Kathleen overheard someone say he was going back to New York on Tuesday. "My heart beat preposterously," she pined.

That Monday, Kathleen went back to that same table, carrying the same book she had been reading, *Le Temple Enseveli (The Buried Temple)* by Maurice Maeterlinck. "Hardly had I settled in the usual place and ordered my meagre meal than [he] passed me and sat down at his usual table." She pretended not to notice. "He glanced at me with his usual half smile, neither less nor more." When Kathleen got up and walked away she could feel him follow in her footsteps.

He reached for her book.

"What are you reading, Esmeralda?" he asked.

"Oh, Maeterlinck," Kathleen replied. "He's good, stick to him."

Steichen told her he had taken a photograph of Maeterlinck and would be happy to give it to her. Later that night he dropped it off at her flat. Before the evening was out he kissed her innocently on the doorstep. "Why didn't I find you before, Esmeralda? You oughtn't be here by yourself, you're not like the others."

Until their meeting, Kathleen had mostly felt alone and discouraged. Steichen changed all that. Although she claims they were just friends his influence would open up her mind and spirit. He was a legitimate artist and would tell her great stories of the masters he knew.

Steichen eventually returned to America. He would be influential in her life again, many years down the road, and for completely different reasons. For now, though, with a fresh new attitude,

Kathleen let Paris surround her. She had an affair with a French painter, seven years her senior, and moved to a place of her own. She started thinking more about her art, both painting and sculpting.

Then she met the "old man."

Steichen had told Kathleen about a picture he had done, a self-portrait that was praised by none other than Auguste Rodin, the great sculptor. He encouraged her to meet him. With a new sense of adventure and self-confidence, Kathleen obliged.

Rodin was sixty-one, Kathleen Bruce only twenty-two, but his studio was close to hers and she visited him often. Hailed for such detailed, life-size statues as *The Age of Bronze* and *The Thinker*, Rodin was later commissioned to make portraits of people. He created nearly a hundred busts in all of painters, writers, and musicians—many of whom he knew well. This made him as popular an artist as he was important. "I would walk with him round his studio," Kathleen wrote. "He would open small drawersused to finding birds eggs in, and show dozens of exquisitely modelled little hands and feet." Often, Rodin came to her flat to have lunch where she fed him fried eggs, bread, and pomegranates. She kept mostly quiet about knowing him, never wanting a mentor, and never suggesting in her memoirs that her friendship with "the old man," as she called him, was anything more than mutual admiration. "Those were days not wasted," she wrote about their time together.

Then in 1903, Rodin intervened in Kathleen's life in a most unusual way. That year a party was being held in Velizy, France, to honor Rodin who had been inducted in the French Legion of Honor. Kathleen would go. On a train from Paris, she discreetly tucked herself into a seat. Excited gasps filled the air. Someone important had just entered, she thought. "I knew no one but became aware that there seemed to be some rather dominant figure around whom the conversation surged." Then she recognized her. "Why yes, it was Isadora Duncan, the great dancer of the day." A few days before, Kathleen and her painter boyfriend had gone to see Miss Duncan dance on a stage backed by an orchestra. "We had both wept unabashedly in our delight," she wrote. Now the famous dancer was next to her. They did not talk. Kathleen was so starstruck that when the train reached the station, she waited until Isadora left the car before leaving her seat.

In Velizy at a restaurant rented by Rodin's friends and students, toasts were made and speeches were given celebrating the man who had become "the greatest sculptor in the world." Isadora Duncan was there. "Somebody said the lovely dancer must dance," Kathleen recalled. Isadora refused at first. Her frock was too long. Someone shouted for her to take it off. She did. Fiddle music began and she danced. When finished, she fell at Rodin's feet. "I was blinded with joy," Kathleen wrote.

Then Rodin brought them together.

He took Isadora's hand and pressed it into Kathleen's.

"My children," he said, "you two should understand each other."

4

Have a cup of tea with us

❧ Around the same time Kathleen Bruce went to Paris, just as the City of Light was attracting talented young artists and writers abroad, America's largest Midwestern city was drawing in businessmen, industrialists, and architects to its ever-expanding skyline. Ever since the Great Fire in 1871, no city its size had seen the type of regrowth Chicago had experienced. Now it rose again, in both infrastructure and people. It was a hub of modern mechanical might and as historian Donald Miller pointed out, "The people visited [Chicago] to witness the forces that would shape the next century." Yet in 1901, within this bustling atmosphere, as curious visitors flocked to the shoreline of Lake Michigan to experience firsthand "the true power and spirit of America," a woman named Mary Desti somehow couldn't wait to leave it.

To be fair, the city wasn't as much the problem for Desti as was her husband, Edward Biden, a traveling salesman. Desti resented being a wife and new mother who was left mostly alone. In January of 1901, she wrapped her son Preston in her arms and started for Paris, abandoning "a disastrous runaway marriage," as she described it.

Desti wasn't going to France blindly. She had been taking voice and acting classes in Chicago and hoped to pursue a career as a stage actress. It's not exactly clear whether she had already set up

lessons in Paris or merely hoped to find her way upon arrival. Regardless, she found herself a young woman with a baby faced with
being a stranger in France. "I didn't know one quarter of Paris
from the other," she admitted.

After arriving in Paris, Desti and the baby stayed in a cold hotel
room trying to keep a fire stoked. She sought to rent a space with
a family where she could have a private room and a piano to study.
She picked up a newspaper in English and found help. "If you
want rooms or apartments or anything, come to Donald Downey,
3 Rue Scribe," read an ad. With Preston bundled in a stroller, she
went to see him.

Donald Downey ran a real estate agency specializing in American transplants looking for residence in Paris. Desti recalled the
visit: the office was small and Mr. Downey was pleasant. "I have
just the very thing for you," he said upon greeting her. "But first
you must come upstairs and meet my wife and have a cup of tea
with us. There is the most delightful American lady with her at
present, whom I am sure you will enjoy meeting."

In an upstairs room above the office was Mrs. Downey making
tea. Next to her was another woman who was "tall and majestic
and lovely," Desti described. She had also rented a room from Mr.
Downey and visited often. Before Desti could speak, the tall woman
approached her with open arms. "Oh, darling, what is your name?"
she asked then turned to little Preston. "Is this yours?" Without
reservation the woman said she had plans for Desti and baby. "Why,
I'm going to take you both right home to meet my daughter."

Although clearly amused by the woman's tenacity, Desti's inten-
tions were clear—she was there to find a place to live. Mr. Downey
obliged, and all three took an automobile to a large house that
had once been owned by a writer and then had been turned into
a school and boarding house for literary and stage artists. It was
inviting with a cozy fire and brightly lit. This is where she would
stay. After paying the month's rent, Desti wished to return to the
office and bid her gracious hosts goodbye. But that "lovely" woman insisted they make one more stop, this time to a studio on Avenue de Villiers. They arrived and climbed a flight of stairs to an

airy room. "Isadora, Isadora, look what I have brought you," the woman cried out. "Mary and her baby."

From another room, Isadora Duncan and her brother Raymond appeared and danced around them both in a circle. "As though I was some person they were waiting for," Desti recalled. Isadora then took Preston and began "gaily playing marvelous dance tunes" on the piano. "At that moment with a great flash of understanding, my heart went out to Isadora," Desti wrote.

Desti left and went to the boarding house room she had just rented. Days later, Preston became feverish. The boarding house turned out to be just as drafty as the cramped hotel room had been. Isadora and her family were the only ones she knew in Paris, so she reached out. Isadora told her to bring the baby over. Within hours, five doctors were attending to Preston. The next morning he was fine. "Your baby is saved," Isadora's mother told her, "but we must get him out of there." Eventually, Mr. Downey found another place for Desti that was "gorgeously furnished," bigger, and more expensive. "I could never afford this," she told him. It was already settled, Downey explained. Isadora, with her mother and brother, would be moving in too.

Later in a book titled *The Untold Story: The Life of Isadora Duncan 1921-1927,* Mary Desti described how her special kinship with Isadora was cemented on that day they first met. "Had I been ushered into paradise and given over to my guardian angel, I could not have been more uplifted." The book was written shortly after Isadora's death in 1927 and is filled with reflections and remembrances of their twenty years together. "How can I with my poor stumbling pen dare to give even the faintest outline of your grace and unearthly beauty," she writes. "How [do you] describe Isadora?"

We'll try.

Isadora Duncan. Hof-Atelier Elvira, photographer, public domain [1904].

5

Fire! Fire! The Windsor's on fire!

✍ Isadora Duncan wasn't just a dancer...she was an enigma. "Always dazzling, always fabulous, she was the personification of flair and anything but ordinary." This is the way Peter Kurth, her principal biographer, described Isadora in a book written in 2001 nearly seventy-five years after her death. Even Kurth, who took nearly a decade to complete the book, admits that while he knew Isadora Duncan the dancer, he knew very little about her life except that she "died famously." And yet there was a BBC film about Isadora from the 1970s titled *The Biggest Dancer in the World,* a movie released earlier in 1968 originally titled *The Loves of Isadora,* and a stage play called *When She Danced.* Vanessa Redgrave played Isadora in both the '60s movie and stage adaptation, and Kurth believes that if more people saw Vanessa as Isadora there wouldn't have been the need for a book. Sadly though, the films and the play are mostly forgotten.

By all indications, Isadora's performances were powerhouse expressions of independence and drama. It wasn't just the dancing, strange as it was, but the whole package she presented. Wearing only a loose-fitting tunic and nothing on her feet, she danced alone, fully exposing herself to the moment and the music. An admirer wrote of her unusual style: "There was no tiptoeing and posturing, no hopeless muscular achievement; all was rhythm, music, light, air, and, above all things, happiness."

Today it would be classified as "modern dance," but at the time it was different, unconventional, somewhat daring, and certainly controversial. "I forbade you to dance to my music," the pianist and composer Ethelbert Nevin once told her. "It isn't dance music. Nobody shall dance it." Then Isadora danced for him. Isadora had sworn to Nevin that if he didn't like her dancing, she would never perform to his music again. "You are an angel," he said apologetically as tears filled his eyes. He not only liked it, but he agreed to do concerts with her.

Isadora claimed her art stemmed from a need to express her "being" in gesture and movement. "As a child I danced the spontaneous joy of growing things," she wrote. This is where her story gets complicated. She was never shy of criticism but also not shy about extolling her own opinion. This often led her down dark paths. She also had great tragedy in her life, and her own death was certainly among the most sudden and bizarre endings ever imagined. History tends to treat Isadora as an anomaly, not quite sure where to classify her among the great performers. "Some will call her blessed," a New York paper once wrote about Isadora and then unkindly implied, "many will call her names."

Isadora's story began in San Francisco in 1871, when her mother, Mary Dora Gray, found a man named Joseph Charles Duncan, who ran a newspaper and a bank. Mary Dora was Joseph's second marriage. He was over fifty. She was almost twenty-one. Isadora came in 1877, the youngest of four siblings: a sister Elizabeth, the eldest, and two brothers, Augustin and Raymond. Isadora didn't remember her father past the age of seven. His bank failed and he left Mary and the children alone. A decade later, Joseph Duncan was dead, killed in a shipwreck. The family eventually moved to Chicago where Isadora danced but made little money. Then they came to New York.

In Manhattan, the Duncans, including Isadora, all moved from a space in Carnegie Hall to the grand Windsor Hotel so they could open up a dancing school, run mostly by sister Elizabeth. For Isadora, now twenty-one, the Nevin concerts led to more intimate salon shows in the homes of New York's wealthiest families, including one hosted by Caroline Webster Shermerhorn Astor, the wife of William Backhouse Astor, Jr., John Jacob Astor, Jr.'s son and heir to his late father's estate.

Mrs. Astor, as she preferred to be called, had a mansion on Bellevue Avenue in Newport, Rhode Island, a retreat for the rich about a hundred miles from New York City. The home included the largest ballroom in town where Isadora danced to an audience of women—mostly wives or widows of men who were famously rich, like the Vanderbilts, perhaps the wealthiest family in the world. Isadora remembered these dances well, but not fondly. "These women were so economical of their cachets," she recalled, "that we hardly made enough to pay the trip and our board." Isadora wanted to move to London, insisting that relocating to Europe meant new artists with whom to mingle and new millionaire men and their wives to fund her groundbreaking work. Yet the thought of such a move was daunting.

That all changed on March 17, 1899, St. Patrick's Day, when Isadora and her mother were helping Elizabeth with an overflow class of thirty aspiring young girls. Suddenly an unexpected thud sounded outside the Windsor's parlor window. Isadora stopped and turned to look. Just then a maid burst into the room. Both Isadora and her mother turned toward the door then back at the window. Mrs. Duncan saw two bodies falling past in a blur. Startled, she turned back and noticed smoke had trailed in with the maid. In the distance, they all heard a man's voice. "Fire! Fire!" he shouted. "The Windsor's on fire!"

Mrs. Duncan, Isadora, and Elizabeth rounded up the girls, wrapped their shoulders in shawls, and calmly led them to the parlor door. "Now children," Mrs. Duncan told them, "the lesson is over. Take hold of hands, and do not on any account let go of each other." They walked in file down the smoky stairs and out the doors where "the little ones were snatched up by willing hands and borne to places of safety," the *New York Times* reported. "Their little hearts were steeled by the encouragement of their teacher."

The account told by the *Times* leaves out Isadora and Elizabeth's role, but it was Elizabeth, according to Isadora, who by "presence of mind" led the girls out safely "hand in hand, Indian style." Regardless of who led the rescue, the girls were shaken but alive. Others weren't so lucky. The hotel was a total loss and the exact death toll (estimated today to be around fifty) was never officially determined.

Although her life was spared, Isadora was a victim too. She lost just about everything in the blaze including her dancing costumes. "This is fate," she said about her sudden predicament. "We must go to London."

Two months later, Isadora and her family were on a cattle boat to England. They settled in Chelsea close to Kensington, known as the Royal Borough of London because Queen Victoria was born there. From the rented, cramped studio they could walk to many of Kensington's important sites including the British Museum, which they frequented often along with the vast Kensington Gardens.

Another smaller garden area was Kensington Square. Filled with blooming flowers in the spring, its bordering streets were lined with some of the finest homes in London. Isadora had danced a little in these great homes and occasionally got paid, but it wasn't enough to make ends meet. "The English are such a polite people," she wrote, but the plaudits ended there. They complimented her costumes and dancing, she added, "But that was all."

Eventually, Elizabeth returned to New York and her dance school, while Raymond and mother Mary Dora stayed with Isadora in London. Times were tough and the money was running out, but Isadora was convinced her big break would come. Then on an Indian summer night in Kensington Square, as Isadora and her brother danced freely in the gardens, an "extremely beautiful woman" dressed in an impeccably fashionable gown and large black hat approached them.

Whether she knew it or not, Isadora was in the presence of one of London's most popular actresses at the time, Beatrice Rose Stella Tanner, known formally by her stage name Mrs. Patrick Campbell or Mrs. Pat for short.

Today, Mrs. Pat's legacy is mostly tied to her often combative friendship and rumored romance with the red-bearded playwright

George Bernard Shaw and the titillating letters they wrote to each other while Shaw was married and Mrs. Pat was a young Boer War widow. "Many thanks for the Friday and Saturday of delightful dreams," Shaw wrote to her lovingly, after a whirlwind twelve hours of private readings in her home for a new play he had written titled *Pygmalion*.

Playing *Pygmalion's* Eliza Doolittle would come later in Mrs. Pat's career. And as history notes, her connection to it is mostly forgotten, overshadowed by the play itself, its controversies, Shaw's legacy, and the success of the 1964 American musical film version titled *My Fair Lady*, starring Audrey Hepburn. "The rain in Spain stays mainly in the plain..."

Before Eliza, however, in 1899, as she enjoyed the peak of her stage popularity, Mrs. Pat stepped out of her home as she often did and went for a walk. She had chosen to live her whole life to that point in one place, stuck to her ways. She was born there and got married there and raised her children there and now as a successful actress had bought a home directly across from an area she loved: Kensington Square.

Her evening strolls in the square were legendary to those who would see her fashionably dressed and gracing them with her presence. One day she noticed someone else. A woman and a man were dancing in the gardens. The woman flowed so beautifully that Mrs. Pat approached them and struck up a conversation.

"Where on earth did you people come from?" she asked.

6

Now I know the meaning of things

◠◡◠ The chance meeting between Mrs. Pat and Isadora Duncan had a profound impact on the life of the young dancer. Isadora was only twenty-two at the time. Mrs. Pat had just turned thirty-four. Mrs. Pat mentioned neither Isadora nor that day in her memoirs. However, Isadora's recollection of meeting Mrs. Pat in Kensington was much more vivid. "We followed her to her lovely home," she wrote. "She sat down and played piano for us, played to us old English songs, and then she recited poetry for us, and I finally danced for her." Isadora was moved by her kindness and transfixed by her grace. "She was magnificently beautiful with luxurious black hair, great black eyes, a creamy complexion, and the throat of a goddess. She made us all fall in love with her."

Mrs. Pat then introduced Isadora to Mrs. Wyndham, the honorable Katherine Cavendish, the wife of George Wyndham, one of Britain's foremost statesman and politicians. "Mrs. Wyndham arranged for me to dance in her drawing room one evening and all the artistic and literary people in London were there," Isadora explained. Then she met a man named Charles Edward Hallé, son of the renowned German musician also named Charles. The elder Hallé was a famed pianist while the son was the director of the New Gallery "where all the modern painters exhibited."

"Modern" was Isadora's game and Hallé knew she fit right in. He invited her to dance at the gallery and soon her life was surrounded by important people, even royalty: the Prince of Wales introduced her to his father, King Edward, who in turn praised her for adding "general enthusiasm to London Society." Isadora was finally getting noticed, and her "fortunes" as she put it, "improved." The Duncans moved into a larger studio, where the dancer welcomed painters, poets and artists—mostly men who understood her work and courted her too.

The family often traveled to Paris where she danced for the French elite. This was around the time Isadora's mother brought Mary Desti and the baby to see her. "Isadora's art was beginning to be greatly appreciated," Desti recalled, "and once or twice a month she gave a recital in her studio in which all the elite among the intelligentsia of Paris came." During one such recital, Desti said she was behind the curtain with Isadora when the music started. Isadora was desperately trying to get a sandal to fit. Realizing she was missing the cue, Desti threw the sandals aside and pushed Isadora on stage, shoeless. "This was the first time that Isadora ever danced barefoot in her life and it created such a sensation, every one raving over the beauty of her feet, that she adopted this forever."

Desti and Isadora were inseparable for nearly a year. Desti studied voice and acting as she had planned and Isadora accompanied her to these lessons, always supportive. They didn't talk about love or men or marriage, Desti recalled. "Isadora was to me like a flower, exquisite and fragile, whose only thought was art." That would change in many explosive ways, but for now Desti had to leave. A message from her mother had abruptly put an end to her time in Paris. Desti and the baby returned to America to tie up loose ends, not the least of which was to finalize a divorce with Preston's good-for-nothing father.

While back in Chicago, Desti sent Edward on his way and re-married—"an old sweetheart," Solomon Sturgis, a wealthy banker, who promptly adopted Preston and gave the boy his last name. Despite being a rich man's wife in a big city, Desti missed the simpler times with Isadora. She convinced her husband to let her spend six months of every year in Europe and take her son Preston with her.

Desti and Isadora's reunion in Germany three years later in 1904 sealed their fate, a friendship that would last a lifetime and for Desti satisfy a constant desire to protect a woman who for better or worse would become entrapped by the lives of the many men whom she let into her life. "Why didn't you tell me about love?" Isadora asked upon seeing her again. "Now I know the meaning of things, music, dancing, everything seems different since the revelations of love. I was born for love."

Indeed, during the three years that Mary Desti was gone, many things had changed in Isadora's life, not the least of which was her sudden stardom. Her barefoot expressive solo dances were all the rage in France, England, and Germany. She would spend many months at a time living in each country, always in fashionable quarters, and always pursed by men. Still there was one man she went to see on her own. Isadora had seen his sculptures firsthand at the 1900 Universal Exhibition in Paris. "Since viewing his work at the Exhibitions, I had been haunted by the sense of Rodin's genius," she wrote.

Unlike the Chicago World's Fair seven years earlier that introduced Rodin to America, the famed sculptor needed no such introductions in France. The exposition in Paris, however, was the first time his collected works were shown together in one place. Isadora went to the Rodin Pavilion to see them.

Isadora approached the sculptor in the way a groupie might approach a rock star today. "My pilgrimage to Rodin," she wrote, "resembled that of Psyche seeking the god Pan in his grotto, only I was not asking the way to Eros, but to Apollo." Rodin was working on a retrospective to debut at the Universal Exposition in Paris at the turn of the century. Isadora was also in Paris.

Their rendezvous that day was revealed for the first time in Isadora's memoirs. It read like a sordid romance novel. Rodin first caressed his statues that "beneath his hands the marble seemed to flow like molten lead," Isadora recalled. Then he took some clay and pressed it between his palms forming a woman's breast. "The heat steamed from him like a radiant furnace," she continued.

Isadora danced and his eyes fixed on her. Then he reached for her. "He ran his hands over my neck, breast, stroked my arms and ran his hands over my hips, my bare legs and feet. He began to knead my whole body like clay, while from him emulated heat that scorched and melted me." Isadora became frightened and withdrew. "I threw my dress over my tunic and sent him away bewildered."

Although Rodin had come on strong in their first meeting, Isadora kept up a correspondence and in 1903 after returning from a successful trip to Berlin went to Velizy on a special train to attend a party in Rodin's honor–the same party attended by the young sculptor Kathleen Bruce. "You too should understand each other," Rodin said bringing the two women together.

7

Thank the gods that I am here

⟡ One of the highlights of a visit to Athens occurs in the early morning when the sun rises over Mount Hymettus sending a "fusion of electric hues" spreading down its limestone slope to the ancient city below. The mountain is literally a skyline, stretching ten miles from Athens to the Saronic Gulf. Strangely flat along its top, it acquired another name from early French travelers during the occupation of Greece: Tréllos or "the crazy one." The highest point is only 3,366 feet. By comparison, it is nearly three times smaller than Mount Olympus and the Mytikas, meaning "nose," which is the highest mountain peak in Greece at nearly ten thousand feet. Still the "crazy" mountain's compressed landscape is unmistakable, though taken for granted in a city that boasts perhaps the most famous rock outcrop in the world.

As the hillocks on Mount Hymettus are traditionally inhabited only by shepherds tending to their goats, it must have been quite a sight when in the early part of the newly turned twentieth century two Americans, a man and a woman, approached these same shepherds to buy some land. These were clearly no goat herders. Upon reaching a rise on the hillside, the man dropped his walking stick and proclaimed in English, "We are on the same level as the Acropolis." It was Raymond Duncan, Isadora Duncan's brother. The woman with him, of course, was Isadora. Indeed the spot looked directly into the east side portals of the Parthenon. The land bore a name, Koponas, given to it by the early settlers.

The sojourn to Greece was Isadora's idea, whose interest in Greek culture and "its mysteries" led to what she described as "a spiritual pilgrimage" to Athens. Also along for the adventure were Isadora's mother, Mary Dora, and a new friend just introduced to her by Rodin, Kathleen Bruce. Kathleen's short entry about the trip in her memoirs explained why she tagged along. "I knew some folk who were going, dancing vagabonds like myself," she wrote, "and joined them there."

For Isadora the sights in Greece were inspiring. She visited ancient Greek temples and took long, deep breaths. "Beauty too sacred for words," she jotted down in her diary. The next day the press found her in the hotel suite resting. "Ah, you cannot imagine how ineffably happy I am in beautiful Athens," she told them. They had visited museums, she added, and got lessons in Greek culture. "I pass my day in Acropolis inhaling inspiration and completing my education."

Someone invariably asked her about dancing. "My dance at present is to lift my hands to the sky to feel the glorious and to thank the gods that I am here," she replied. While in Greece, Isadora bought the plot of land in Koponas and set out to build a "temple" dedicated to Hellenism, an old ancient Greek worship of the gods. Isadora had great plans for it. "We were to greet the rising sun with joyous songs and dances," she wrote. "The afternoons were to be spent in meditation, and the evenings given over to pagan ceremonies."

When the "vagabonds" returned to Europe, Isadora kept a busy schedule with tours in Vienna, Berlin, and Paris before returning to London. The next year she and her mother moved to Berlin while Raymond stayed in Greece to help build the temple, something Isadora had wished she could do as well, but could not because of a commitment to a dancing tour in Germany. From there they traveled to Budapest and Poland. Kathleen Bruce went too. The two women had connected since meeting in Paris and the trip to Greece was a joy.

Isadora was already famous when she met Kathleen, so Kathleen's role in her life would be mostly supportive. Like Mary Desti, Kathleen would be a friend and companion, someone with whom Isadora could confide in time of need. But before she met them both, there was another artist, another dancer in fact, whose influence was invaluable to Isadora. And it all started at the same place Isadora saw Rodin's work for the first time.

8

It's a butterfly.
A butterfly!

◯ In the final days of the 1900 Paris Exhibition, on Saturday, November 3, inside a quaint building that sat beside a grove of horse chestnut trees on the Rue de Paris, Japanese actress Kawakami Sadayakko, known as Sada Yacco, walked offstage one last time to uproarious applause. The accolades were warranted for continuity alone. Yacco and the Japanese troupe had just wrapped up an astounding 369 performances in 123 days.

In the wings, overseeing the act was an American woman named Loie Fuller. Fuller was popular for her own solo dance, one uniquely highlighted by reflective backgrounds and electrical, colored lights. "She oozed brightness," one critic enthused. However, at the exhibition, Fuller limited her dancing. Yacco was clearly the star. "There certainly was a 'clou' to the exhibition of 1900," a French journalist named Louis Fournie explained. "It was not a great mechanical enterprise, or a tower erected. [The Eiffel Tower had been introduced at the 1889 fair.] It was a woman—Madame Sada Yacco."

Yacco had been dancing since the age of four and at fifteen, like other young Japanese teenagers, became a geisha. As tradition dictated, this was followed shortly by the young girl's parents selling their geisha daughter's virginity to the highest bidder. In Yacco's case it was the prime minister of Japan. Released from his hold three years later, she began acting and soon met her husband, another stage actor, Kawakami Otojiro, known as "The Liberty Kid." They took their act to America where they translated famous Asian works for Western audiences. When Yacco came to Paris at the turn of the century, she had established a name and a following. "I turned Sada Yacco loose," Fuller would later recall about Yacco's performances at the Expo.

Next the troupe set out on a whirlwind tour of major cities like Tokyo, London, and Glasgow before returning to Paris in August 1901. Yacco's reappearance this time in a "fashionable" theater was all the rage. Fuller decided to make promotional posters of Yacco's return visit. She was given an address for a young Spanish artist who was getting notice not just for the quality of his work but also the speed and quantity by which he produced it. Fuller was assured he had done posters and illustrations for some of France's most famous cabaret stars, and so she and Yacco went to see him. The young man—only nineteen at the time—was Pablo Picasso.

The poster Picasso painted of Yacco is no great masterpiece. In fact, one Picasso expert called it "uninspiring." But in retrospect it shows a budding master carefully crafting his work, in this case a dramatic death scene. Yacco is portrayed looking down with her hands up in the air. In her right hand is a knife. Her kimono is bloodied. Her face shows no expression. Its simplicity is its reward, but by all accounts Fuller didn't care much for it. To her, a bronze sculpture she commissioned of Yacco's head, life-size in her traditional courtesan headdress, was more impressive. The name of that artist was Bernstein.

Isadora first saw Yacco dance at the Expo, but she met Fuller during the second Paris run. In Isadora's account, it was the American soprano Emma Nevada who brought them together. "She is not only a great artist but she is such a pure woman," Nevada remarked about Fuller. Nevada was dating Isadora's brother Raymond at the time and suggested Isadora see the American dancer. Perhaps the international star could help propel her career even further. Isadora finally got to see Fuller dance. "Before my eyes," she wrote, "she turned from many-coloured, shining orchids, to a wavering, flowering sea-flower. What an extraordinary genius!"

Sada Yacco. Unknown photographer. Public domain in Japan and U.S.

Loie Fuller. Wikimedia Commons, public domain [1892].

Born on a farm in Hinsdale, Illinois, just outside of Chicago, Loie Fuller's life of dance started at an early age. As she tells the story, when only six weeks old her mother brought her to a neighbor's house where a group of traveling dancers were performing. Mrs. Fuller had nowhere else to take the baby so she brought little Loie along hoping she would sleep quietly in a back room. The infant had other ideas. When the music started, two men heard a racket coming from the room. When they entered the baby was moving about, or as they put it "agitating her feet and hands in every direction." The dancers were so impressed they passed the little girl around while performing. The baby became the main attraction. "That is how I made my debut," Fuller recalls, "at the age of six weeks."

As silly as that sounds, Fuller did keep performing. Her first stage appearance was reciting a poem at the age of three. "Despite the mistakes I made, the spirit of it was intelligible and impressed the audience," she recalled.

When she grew up, acting and dancing became her focus. Her most famous act called the "Serpentine dance" came by accident. While performing in a drama titled *Quack MD,* Fuller played a young widow who was hypnotized by a doctor. Before opening night, Fuller asked the electrician to put green footlights on the stage to create the visual effect of her being in a trance. Fuller needed something to wear and found a silk skirt at the bottom of her dressing trunk. The material was sheer and "comparable to a spider's web," she remembers. When the play opened, the hallucination scene was a hit. While the stage was illuminated in a green glow, Fuller danced. "I endeavored to make myself as light as possible in order to give the impression of a fluttering figure, obedient to the doctor's orders." The dress was broad enough on the bottom that she kept tripping on it. So Fuller grabbed the ends and fanned out her arms lifting the material like wings along her sides. It was an instant sensation.

"It's a butterfly. A butterfly!" someone in the house shouted.

After *Quack MD's* run ended, Fuller had mostly given up on wearing the sheer dress again. She brought it home to fix a tear and when she tried it on again, the light coming through the windows' curtains cast an amber glow in the room. The translucent effect upon the dress was even more stunningly beautiful than the stage lights. "Unconsciously, I realized that I was in the presence of a great discovery, one which was destined to open the path, which I have since followed, I had created a new dance."

What followed was a stage act unlike anything anyone had seen before. "A whirling, spinning, incandescent floor show," as one writer described, "that left audiences gasping and poets, painters, and fashion designers straining to capture its effects."

Isadora was swept up in it too. "She transformed herself into a thousand colorful images before the eyes of her audience," she wrote about Fuller. "I was carried away by this marvelous artist." Fuller was just as enthralled with Isadora's art. "She danced with remarkable grace, her body barely covered...and she bade fair to become somebody. To me it was the most beautiful thing in the world. Oh, how I loved it."

Fuller then made Isadora an offer to join her and Sada Yacco for concerts in Berlin. This was a wholly new experience for Isadora. Fuller traveled with an entourage, including the other women dancers who adored her to the point of infatuation. "I was completely taken aback by this, by coming upon this extreme attitude of expressed affection," Isadora lamented. "It was all quite new to me."

Yacco was different. "She was shy, reticent, with a finely molded yet strong face, black hair brushed straight back from her forehead, with sad and intelligent eyes." Isadora felt Yacco was someone to whom she could connect. But Yacco was too focused on her work, and her devotion to Fuller "possessed her entire emotional force and left nothing for me," Isadora remarked.

Despite being ill for most of the run in Berlin, Isadora recovered in time for a successful tour in Vienna. There she danced for Austria's Princess Pauline Metternich, as well as the British and American ambassadors to Vienna, writers and artists, and a slew of journalists. Afterward Fuller was invited to see the princess. "Why does she [Isadora] dance so insufficiently clothed?" the princess asked.

"It was an accident," Fuller lied.

She explained that Isadora's dancing costume had not yet arrived and she went on stage in just her practice outfit, a simple tunic, which did not hide much, especially her breasts. While the princess may have had concerns, the audiences that followed were clearly enthralled by the "naked, barefooted nymph," as one writer described her. Isadora's stardom rose quickly, soon surpassing the enthusiasm for Fuller and even the alluring Yacco.

What happened next is related from two completely different perspectives. Fuller claims Isadora abandoned her at the height of her success without a "word of thanks or a goodbye." For Isadora, it was more loneliness than spite, although she did come to resent how the other dancers grouped about Loie. In the end, however, it was her mother back in Paris she missed the most.

Simply put, Isadora's name was as well-known as Loie Fuller's, and Fuller wasn't dancing much anymore due to chronic back pain. The torch was passed. That, at least, was Isadora's final assessment of the matter. Years later, Isadora would fondly recall her launch into international stardom. "Mrs. Pat" may have introduced her to important and influential artists in London, but Loie Fuller made Isadora a name, not just in England, but in all of Europe.

Now blessed with a new friend in sculptor Kathleen Bruce and a constant companion in Mary Desti, Isadora's personal life was just as fulfilling as her professional one. Personally, both Kathleen and Mary would go on to support Isadora as she worked through complicated relationships with men, motherhood, and then eventually an unspeakable tragedy. Professionally, though, while on a roll in London and Europe, fame continued to elude her at home. That would soon change, however, thanks to one man in America who had big plans in mind for the famous dancer.

Mildred Morris as Wendy and Maude Adams as Peter Pan. From the Bruce K. Hanson collection, courtesy of Bruce K. Hanson.

Act II

౭⁄⊘ "I regard the theatre as the greatest of all art forms, the most immediate way in which a human being can share with another the sense of what it is to be a human being." –*Oscar Wilde*

Charles Frohman sat at his desk and then sprung up again and nervously paced the spacious office he occupied directly above the theater he managed, the Empire on New York's Broadway Street.

As an impresario and one of New York's most prolific producers, Frohman had many days like this, pacing his office and anxiously awaiting word of a play that had just opened at one of his theaters. This time it was in London at the Duke of York's Theatre in the city's West End. When the curtain rose on the production there, it was 8:30 P.M. In New York, it was early afternoon.

Frohman was anticipating a cable to arrive with word on how this new production, one he had personally cast and groomed, would be received.

Even before the opening in London, Frohman had begun preparations for the show to run in America at the Empire Theatre the following December.

He was convinced it would be a hit.

But first that cable.

"Will it never come?" Frohman muttered. Finally, it did. A message from his London business partner William Lestocq.

It was exactly what Frohman had hoped for.

"PETER PAN ALL RIGHT," the cable proclaimed. "LOOKS LIKE A BIG SUCCESS."

1

My God! Don't do it! Don't do it!

⤲ Just after 3:00 A.M. on March 13th, 1906, actor Louie De Lange was spotted returning to his room at the Mock's Hotel in the 100 block of New York's 42nd Street, seemingly drunk, and accompanied by two other men. Several hours later, De Lange's body was found in his bed, dead, his throat cut from one end to the other. Next to a mirror was a bloody razor.

No one seemed to suspect foul play. "Playwright Takes Own Life" the dispatches from New York read the next day. In the paper, De Lange's brother gave a plausible reason why De Lange might consider such an act. De Lange had been in a few plays, most notably *Quack MD* with actress Loie Fuller, but he had not been working much since. In addition, he had just sent his wife and two-year-old child to live in a sanatorium on Long Island.

Then the story of two other men emerged. Now there was curiosity at least. Witnesses at the hotel could only describe the two men, unknown to them, as one likely being De Lange's cabman and the other, as it would turn out, a young newspaper boy, who shortly before had sold De Lange the morning paper. "I would not go on record as saying that this is not a case of murder," the coroner who examined the body, a man named Shrady, remarked. "The cut in the throat is not high up and close to the chin as it nearly always is in cases of suicide. But nevertheless, the nature of the wound is such that it might have been made by the victim as well as by another."

The newspaper boy, Samuel Kerman, only seventeen, was identified. He was arrested and questioned. Kerman did not dispute he was with the playwright that night but it was only to pick up a package that Mr. De Lange wanted him to deliver. There was nothing nefarious about the visit other than the unusual time that it took place. When he left, De Lange was very much alive.

There was something else police were suspicious about. A hotel maid said she heard De Lange's voice coming from the room shouting, "My God! Don't do it! Don't do it!" Could the boy explain that? He could not. Also missing from the victim's room was money and an expensive watch. Any explanation as to the whereabouts? Again, there was no response. Lack of evidence and frustration would eventually send Kerman home. He was never charged and the case remained unsolved. As Loie Fuller remembered it, De Lange's death was a mystery, and so it would remain.

Perhaps even more shocking was where the incident took place. Mock's Hotel was on 42nd street, one of New York's most famous cross streets, and, at the corner of Broadway, one of the most brightly lit too. Situated in an area once known as Beavers Square in the early 1800s, like most of New York's streets, 42nd followed a map path that once flowed a series of streams stemming from and branching out of the Hudson River. The site was a dumping ground for horse manure until the stream was filled in and farmers sensing the rich soil began settling there. What was once over three hundred streams covering sixty-six miles is now modern-day Manhattan. One stream called the Great Kill is essentially today's 42nd Street. (The "kill" in this instance being Dutch for streams or channels.) Based on what occurred in the Mock's Hotel nearly a century later, the name proved apt enough.

But it's not as if Broadway, like many other streets in the urban landscape of a big city like New York, lacked its share of indecorous behavior. One such incident took place on the steps of the luxurious Astor House Hotel built by mogul William B. Astor on land owned by his father, the fur trader millionaire, John Jacob Astor. The six-story, granite-walled Astor House stood next to St.

Paul's church to the right and faced City Hall across the street. The hotel's steps were decoratively columned giving it a grand entrance. This opulence made the setting even more disturbing when on November 1, 1843, a murder nearly took place. Officially it was an attempted murder, since the victim, a man named Henry Ballard, a sales merchant who stayed at the hotel, lived to tell the tale. The suspected killer, he proclaimed, was his mistress. The mistress was Amelia Norman. She stabbed Ballard with a folding pocketknife that day, clearly intending to kill him. The trial that followed was one of the most talked about in the nation thanks to the sensationalist nature of the act. Ballard was portrayed as a two-timing seducer who, when he and Norman had a baby together, refused to offer any support to her or the child. Ballard's charge was jealousy on the part of his mistress. When the jury verdict was announced, thousands filled the streets in support of Norman whose revenge of being wronged by a man was justified in the public eye and now deemed unpunishable by the court. She was acquitted in just ten minutes.

Despite these transgressions, Manhattan's entertainment district was thriving thanks to visionaries like the aforementioned John Jacob Astor and partner William Cutting who purchased the land between 42nd and 47th Streets near the banks of the Hudson River so they could expand their lucrative fur trade. The Astors would become one of New York's wealthiest families, and the dirt land Astor once owned off 42nd Street that cut a diagonal path across the city is now the Broadway of today, home of the most famous theater-district street in the world.

2
Someday I will be an impresario

~~⁓~~ Before the theaters arrived, stables, schools, and churches dotted Broadway Street. Then motorized vehicles began replacing horses, and the carriage companies moved out. The theaters moved too, coming uptown and leaving an area near City Hall to settle where the horse businesses used to be. At first it was just the acting companies that resettled, but then the theaters came, all bearing the names of the men who envisioned them.

One man named T. Henry French is widely credited with "building the Broadway." The first palace he built, properly named the Broadway Theatre, seated nearly two thousand patrons and had a seventy-five-foot-wide stage. Two more theaters followed including the Metropolitan Opera House which burnt down in 1892 and then was rebuilt. In 1966, it was moved to its current location in Lincoln Center, but it began on Broadway.

Based on his success on Broadway, French built an even bigger stage on 42nd Street. This one would have a combination main auditorium and roof garden stage that at ninety feet was wider than the stage in the Broadway Theatre. French's American Theatre was completed in 1893 and the first production was a London import titled *The Prodigal Daughter*. As a debut, it was quite a spectacle. The cast numbered two hundred and included nine racehorses featured in a wild steeplechase scene where the animals ran on a moving treadmill and jumped over constructed water hazards and hurdles. The horses weren't always good actors. One named Columbus stumbled at a hurdle and nearly crushed its rider. Another rambunctious mare, Rochefort, tried to escape by leaping over an iron gate, causing the leading lady to faint in horror. "Far as I know, the horses behaved according to script," a theater magazine writer George Odell joked about the scene. Either despite or due to the ruckus, the play was a literally and figuratively a smash and French's theater a success.

In 1895, another influential theater manager, Oscar Hammerstein I, opened his Olympia Theatre complex on Broadway between 44th and 45th Streets. Here Loie Fuller starred with Louie De Lange in *Quack MD*. Hammerstein's complex had its share of challenges, but as an entertainment hub it drew in more patrons. Today, the Hammerstein name is remembered mostly due to Oscar Hammerstein II, the grandson of Hammerstein I, whose string of hit shows with partner Richard Rodgers made the duo of Rodgers and Hammerstein the most successful partnership in musical theater. Until then, though, the patron of the family, the first Oscar Hammerstein, was considered one of the most important figures, if not "the most important," according to some historians, in the emergence of New York's theater scene.

Born in Germany, Oscar Hammerstein's love of theater, specifically operas, began in Berlin as a child. When he came to America in 1863 at age fifteen, he began working in a cigar factory for two dollars a week. The educated Hammerstein soon established himself as more than just an immigrant laborer. He offered up new ideas and gadgets to his boss since his current status did not allow him to apply for patents himself. That would change nine years later when Hammerstein finally became a U.S. citizen. His first patent for a multiple cigar mold earned him enough money to start up a successful cigar trade journal called *The Tobacco Journal,* which included listings of local tobacconists who paid Hammerstein for the privilege to advertise their wares to wholesalers and other retailers.

When a friend asked him to help open a theater named the Germania, Hammerstein jumped right in, not only guaranteeing

Oscar Hammerstein I. The Library of Congress, part of the the Bain Collection [1908].

financing but also producing several plays that he wrote. Around this same time, he married a woman named Rose Blau. They had four sons together, all of whom grew up to work for their father in the theater business. More cigar patents followed, and Hammerstein began buying property and building apartment houses on 7th Avenue near 135th Street in an area then known for its middle-class residences that went by the name that it still does today: Harlem.

This is when Hammerstein began thinking of the operas he loved as a boy. He sold the cigar journal and built an opera house. The Harlem Opera House was a mild success thanks to its stars, including one of New York's most popular actors at the time, Edwin Booth, the brother of President Lincoln's assassin, John Wilkes Booth. Despite denouncing his estranged brother's treasonous act, Edwin Booth still had to go into exile for a time before reappearing on stage again as Hamlet, his favorite character. Because Hammerstein's theater was so far uptown, and most of the performers lived closer to the theaters on Broadway, Booth and others asked for high salaries to compensate, and Hammerstein paid them. One popular actor named Joseph Jefferson reportedly demanded 90 percent of the gross.

While the house was packed, Hammerstein still had trouble paying the bills. He did have a reserve plan though. Another cigar invention and another sold patent—this time for $65,000—kept the theater open. So far Hammerstein had presented mostly dramas with an occasional opera mixed in. His inability to book operas was not entirely his fault. By this time, the Metropolitan Opera House had established itself on Broadway as the premier opera house in New York and management denied Hammerstein's request to bring the stars to Harlem. Hammerstein improvised. He found his own stars and created his own company. "Someday I will be an impresario," he determinedly told his composer Walter Damrosch.

Hammerstein reached deep into his pockets and built two more theaters, including the Columbus in Harlem and the Manhattan Opera House in Herald Square. Named for the building that housed the *New York Herald,* it was located at Broadway and 34th Street not far from the Met. Hammerstein was now truly in the opera game. The first production of *Lena Despard,* which opened on November 15, 1892, starring the heralded English actress Fanny Bernard Barre, known by her stage name Mrs. Bernard Barre, and making her American debut. "Mrs. Barre will have an attentive hearing," the *New York Times* predicted in a preview.

But when the curtain dropped on the first night, the production of *Lena Despard,* an interpretation of Francis Charles Philips's novel *As in the Looking Glass,* was panned. "Mrs. Barre's vehicle contains more talk than action," the papers read, "and is overburdened by absurd soliloquies that seem like interpolated parenthesis here and there for a confidential explanation to the audience."

The star was rather the opera house itself, and Hammerstein was given credit for creating a theater "that the public desires." Innovations included a drop curtain, traditionally a solid piece of heavy cloth, now instead cut down the middle. This made curtain calls easier, the paper noted. The first two balconies extended far over the auditorium "giving a direct and near view of the performance."

But looks and comfort could not sustain a theater presenting operas alone, and there was still only one successful opera house in New York. To offset the cost of the opera productions, Hammerstein hired two vaudeville performers named John Koster and Albert Bial to oversee weekly musical send-ups in the theater. "Koster and Bial's Music Hall" as it was presented was an instant success, and Hammerstein would have likely ridden its coattails had greed, jealousy, and ego not intervened.

Hammerstein was approached by a man named George Kessler who was the New York seller for Moët & Chandon champagne. Kessler had a favor to ask. Could Hammerstein see to presenting a singer he knew, a woman named Marietta del Rio, who was represented by a French firm Kessler was doing business with overseas? Hammerstein apparently didn't care much for Kessler and declined. Kessler then went to Koster and Bial who were upset with Hammerstein over an embarrassing production titled *The Kohinoor* that Hammerstein on a bet had written himself and made them produce. The crowd had roared with laughter, but laughter was not what Hammerstein intended. Koster and Bial felt they would be scapegoats if the play failed. The play failed. So, when

Kessler went behind Hammerstein's back and presented the idea of del Rio directly to Koster and Bial, they jumped at the chance. As the story goes, on opening night when del Rio came out, Hammerstein stood up and booed (some reports claim he booed and hissed).

Kessler was seated in the same box not far away. Suddenly the real show was in the balcony. The two men lunged at each other and threw punches in a fight that carried out to the corridor and onto the street. Police were called and both men were arrested. Koster and Bial posted bail on behalf of Kessler and left Hammerstein in jail. Their plan was to force Hammerstein to give up control of the theater, but it didn't quite work that way. Hammerstein was bailed out by a friend and promptly sued Koster and Bial for damages and misconduct. The case dragged on and posed potentially damaging press for the vaudeville duo. Hammerstein used it as leverage.

The judge announced a decision, fair or otherwise. It boiled down to this: Hammerstein had a right to boo someone in his own theater. Koster and Bial knew it. They settled and paid nearly $340,000 to Hammerstein partially to buy him out and partially to stay in business. Hammerstein signed the papers and reportedly told them, "When I get through with you, everybody will forget there ever was a Koster and Bial's. I will build a house the likes of which has never been seen in the whole world." As one writer explained, "Hammerstein took that [settlement] money and an additional $2 million and changed history."

In this case the history-changing moment was the opening of the Olympia Theatre complex on Broadway. The four theaters were the largest theater group of its kind and while it was not as successful as Hammerstein had hoped, it did draw more attention to what would become known as New York's Theater District, an area originally called Longacre Square, but today known as the iconic Times Square.

Hammerstein's sons were all successful in the business, including William who became an impresario in his own right. William managed one of his father's most successful theaters, the Victoria on 42nd Street. Willie, as he was known, wasn't as much in love with the theater as he was in giving the audience a good show. He introduced bizarre theatrical spectacles like the Cherry Sisters, a singing trio, billed as "America's worst act." He staged a contest where comedians tried to make a woman named Sober Sue laugh –Willie didn't tell them that Sober Sue's face was permanently paralyzed by illness. After one performance, he even arranged for his own dancers to be arrested for indecent exposure.

His most egregious stunt involved the actress Evelyn Nesbit, known as "the Girl on the Velvet Swing." Willie was suspected of protecting Nesbit from her husband Harry K. Thaw who was convicted of killing another man, Stanford White, with whom Nesbit may have had an affair. "So long as Harry Thaw is alive and free, I shall never close my eyes in peace," Nesbit told a reporter for the *New York Herald* shortly after news broke that Thaw had escaped from prison. Willie provided Nesbit with a police escort and in return devilishly set the stage for a possible confrontation. *Might the escaped Thaw show up at one of Evelyn Nesbit's performances?* Willie had a way of filling the seats, however deviously the plan was hatched.

Willie died of illness in 1914, at the age of forty-one. "Hammerstein, the Barnum of vaudeville is dead," the *Times* declared. He never lived to see his son Oscar rise to greatness with stalwart Rodgers and Hammerstein productions such as *Showboat, Oklahoma, Carousel, The King and I,* and *The Sound of Music.* It is said that shortly before his death, Willie made his brother Arthur, another producer, promise him to not let Oscar, who was nineteen when his father passed, get into the theater business–a promise, Arthur fortunately did not keep.

In history's long view, the patriarch Oscar Hammerstein I, by virtue of his name and namesake, is mostly lost behind his son's antics and his grandson's success. Still he is not completely forgotten. "He has done more for music than other man in America," the patriotic bandleader John Philip Sousa would say about Hammerstein in 1919, shortly after the impresario's death at the age of seventy-two. The *New York Times* obituary was even more complimentary: "The restless energy of his mind and his inexhaust-

Evelyn Nesbit Thaw. The Library of Congress, part of the Genthe Collection [1913-1942].

ible fertility of invention made him, during one brief period, the regenerator of our musical life." One book written in 1991 about the history of Broadway even dubs Hammerstein "The Father of Times Square."

Not far down the road from Hammerstein's original Olympia Theatre complex sits the Empire Theatre at Broadway and 40th Street. Built around the same time, the Empire was the brainchild of another mostly forgotten entertainment impresario who went on to become one of the most important and influential men of the theater in the early twentieth century: Charles Frohman.

3

But, Charles, this is not a theater

༄ Before we examine Charles Frohman, let's first backtrack to the start of the Empire Theatre, one of the most famous and successful buildings on Broadway. The story of the Empire, though, can't be told without introducing another influential theater producer of the time, David Belasco.

Belasco began his theater career in San Francisco as an actor and play adapter. Having a few productions under his belt, Belasco moved to New York in 1880 to work as a playwright. Belasco wrote melodramas, an actor's dream because they were wordy and required facial expressions and movements to carry the dramatic weight of the story along. Basically, there was little to look at beyond the actors and their glances. But that would change. Lighting proved a good start. Belasco was one of the first to experiment with it, creating his proudest effect—a sunset—along with other mood setters simply by changing the color or tone.

Actors liked to work for Belasco because he was once an actor himself. He knew what motivated them. In one unusual but effective method, Belasco would feign a temper tantrum when he felt the crew was being lackadaisical. He would reach into his pocket, take out his watch, and slam it to the floor, shattering it to pieces. The stunned cast would be galvanized into a more productive day.

Unbeknownst to them, Belasco always kept a box in his office filled with cheap, dime-store watches.

Belasco built his first theater in 1902 and then in 1907 built a palace, originally named the Stuyvesant Theatre but then changed to the Belasco Theatre three years later. The Belasco was impressive from its elevator stage to "the most complete lighting setup of any theater at the time," according to a book on the history of Broadway. Though it was "somewhat off the beaten path" on 44th Street just off Sixth Avenue, nonetheless it was successful. Belasco had a string of hits including a play he opened at two theaters at the same time. The dual performances of Ferenc Molnar's *The Devil* opened on the same day in 1908, both playing to packed houses. The Belasco Theatre was just far enough away from the Garden Theatre to suggest the audience's choice was based on location, but in reality it was more a preference over which prominent actor they preferred to see perform.

Long before he had success with the Belasco Theatre, however, when Belasco was still writing more plays than staging them, he sought out a producer who was just making a name for himself on Broadway.

That man was Charles Frohman.

Charles Frohman's love for the theater began early. At the age of seven he attended a play called *The Black Crook* on Lower Broadway. So entranced by the drama unfolding on the stage, he missed a family-imposed curfew. Scurrying home after the final curtain, he reached the door and was greeted by his mother. She was not pleased. Charles, however, was ecstatic. "I have seen a play," he told her. "It was wonderful."

Growing up on Third Street just off Broadway, Charles would walk to the theaters and marvel at the large billboards announcing the latest shows and stars. His middle brother Gustave got even closer. Gustave found a job selling opera books at the Academy of Music on Fourteenth Street and let Charles tag along. Charles stood outside and watched as the highbrow-types shuffled into the lobby and bought books from his brother. Charles asked if he could

David Belasco. The Library of Congress, part of the Bain Collection.

do the same. "You're not even a teenager," his brother explained; it would have to wait. Charles nagged his brother every day until Gustave finally gave in. Charles had his chance. The first day he sold one book and only made seventeen cents, but he was in a theater.

Charles sold books and posters, finally getting a job working in the box office booth at Hooley's Theatre in Brooklyn when he was just fourteen. The oldest of the three Frohman brothers, Daniel also got into the business as an agent. One day Daniel was billing a show at the Woods Theatre and Charles offered to help. He proceeded to place posters in high travel areas and the show sold out. Daniel took notice, but it was Gustave that got him his first true theater job, managing a struggling traveling theater company that had just started a tour in the Midwest.

In 1881, Charles, now twenty-five, returned to New York and along with his two brothers ran bookings and productions for the Madison Square Theatre, a small playhouse located at the back of the Fifth Avenue Hotel. The three Frohman brothers handled every aspect of the operation: Gustave directed the traveling companies, Daniel hired the cast and organized rehearsals, and Charles arranged and booked the road tours.

Charles started thinking bigger. He wanted to manage a theater on his own. In 1883 he found a barnlike structure near 35th and Broadway that was used as a skating rink among other things. David Belasco had written a play that Charles was interested in producing called *The Stranglers of Paris*. The rest of the theater houses were all booked.

"This is all I can get," Charles told Belasco about the skating rink.

Belasco balked. "But, Charles, this is not a theater."

"Never mind," Charles said, "I will make it into one."

Another theater down the street was closing and Charles convinced the owner to let him have the old proscenium arch. It was a start. Charles had a stage at least.

The Stranglers of Paris opened on November 8, 1883, to a warm reception. One of its stars was John Bunny, a portly comic who would later gain fame in the movies. Henry Lee was another actor whose successful career started with *Stranglers*. Also included in

Charles Frohman. New York Public Library, from the Billy Rose Theater Division.

the cast was Agnes Booth, the recently widowed wife of Junius Brutus Booth and sister-in-law of the popular New York stage actor Edwin Booth. *Stranglers of Paris* was a turning point for Frohman who started focusing on producing plays rather than just booking them. That year he officially broke away from his two brothers and became an independent manager.

Frohman began to market shows for other theater troupes that had been staging productions only seen by New Yorkers. Frohman thought the shows would be just as popular throughout the country. While on one such tour in Portland, Oregon, a railroad agent approached him at the station. "I want you to meet a very promising young actress who is out here with her mother." The actress turned out to be Maude Adams. Frohman would remember her.

Several years later in 1892, the New York theater scene was at a crossroads. Most of its established and popular actors, like Edwin Booth, were either passing away or retiring. Frohman seized on the opportunity to promote a new lineup of stars. John Drew was one. Drew wasn't new to the theater, but instead was a well-known circuit actor. Frohman cleverly signed him to a three-year contract, giving him exclusive rights to an established name. Maude Adams was another. She was new. Drew and Adams made their first appearance together in Frohman's *The Masked Ball* at the Plymouth Theatre. It was a massive success, not just for the producer but for the leading actress too. The consensus was that Maude Adams was Frohman's next big star.

As Frohman's status grew so did his desire to own a theater of his own. A dream he had since first stepping into one, Frohman waited to see what would become available. Then in 1892, a theater producer from Boston named William Harris intervened: "Charley, I want a theater in New York and I know that you want one. Let's combine."

"You can have the Union Square Theatre," Frohman told Harris. "The lease is on the market." When Frohman told another friend, a man named Al Hayman, about Harris's offer, Hayman laughed it off. "That's foolish," Hayman told Frohman. "Everything theatrical is going uptown." Hayman had an idea. He owned several lots at 40th and Broadway. "I will build one for you" he said.

On January 25, 1893, the Empire Theatre opened its doors and Frohman had his theater. His first proclamation would be one of his most enduring. That day, Frohman was told there were no electric lights hung in the auditorium. "The Empire opens tonight," he declared, "even if we have to open it by candlelight." The lights were installed, the show went on, and Frohman earned a reputation for never postponing an opening. He immediately set up an office on the Empire's third floor. Stock in the enterprise grew, and soon Frohman was wealthy enough to buy interest in more theaters.

He had conquered New York.

London was next.

4

I'm just looking

✑ In the mid-nineteenth century, London's equivalent to
New York's Theater District was the West End, which covered
a wide swath of land. But unlike its American counterpart, London's roads swooped and swerved so no one street in the West
End was clearly distinguishable as being the main street, like New
York's Broadway Street. Oxford, Regent, and Strand Streets, perhaps, came the closest. In a map of the West End from 1860, fifteen theater houses are listed, but only two have addresses that
share the same street. The largest cluster of theaters stood in the
far eastern section of the West End closest to the River Thames
near Strand Street, which ran parallel to the river, and Wellington Street, which led to the Waterloo Bridge. "You must not take
the theaters too far west," wrote the playwright Dion Boucicault,
"it must be in the centre of the pleasure-seeking population."

The farthest theater west on Oxford Street was named the Princess. It staged Boucicault's *The Corsican Brothers,* a play that would
become famous and in turn aggrandize the theater for the last
scene of the first act. That's when an actor playing the two main
roles of the Corsican brothers (separated throughout by distance
in the play), appear to be actually on stage together, a deception
created by using a quick-switch exit and a system of man-powered
pulleys leading to a trapdoor on the stage. While the audience was

tricked into thinking the brother, now a concealed stage double, had remained on stage, the other brother, clearly the actor, magically appears in apparition form from the back, bloodied as if dead from an assassin's bullet. The ghost waves his arms to reveal a forest whereby he shows his brother the killer, in this case a fellow duelist, who must be avenged (hence Act Two). The curtain falls on intermission before the stunned audience can figure it all out. Even Queen Victoria was so enthralled and baffled by the deception that she saw the play four times.

By 1892, London's theater district grew to include the Duke of York's Theatre on St. Martin's Lane. This is where Charles Frohman would stage his most popular productions. "If you want to know the character of my repertory project at the Duke of York's, I should describe it as the production of new plays by living authors," Frohman announced upon his arrival to the London scene.

Frohman however wasn't the only American looking to make his mark in London. Another man, Harry Selfridge, came looking for success on Oxford Street as well. Although not in the entertainment business himself, his impact would have a ripple effect on the West End as a whole. He would also have an indirect but important influence on the lives of Frohman and others.

Harry Gordon Selfridge was born in Ripon, Wisconsin, a small town eighty miles northwest of Milwaukee. Harry's father, Robert Oliver Selfridge, owned a dry-goods store in Ripon before moving the family to Tecumseh, Michigan, a nod to his wife Lois's wishes to be closer to her relatives. Shortly after arriving in Tecumseh in 1861, Robert enlisted in the Third Michigan Cavalry. He never came back. Tragically, while he was away, death came at home too. Both of Harry's brothers, Charles and Robert, Jr., died of illness. Only Harry at twelve years old was left. Lois took her only surviving son away from the sickness and grief in Tecumseh and moved to Jackson, Michigan, instead.

When he was old enough, Harry got a job in a bank to care for his mother. He refused an appointment to Annapolis and toyed with becoming a lawyer. That thought was short-lived. Instead, he took a menial job in a grocery store. As his late father did, Harry

Harry Gordon Selfridge while at Marshall Field's in Chicago. "The Life and Times of Harry Gordon Selfridge", public domain.

dreamed of owning his own merchant store. That's when he met merchant owner Leonard Field who directed Harry to his cousin Marshall, another successful merchant who had just opened a dry-goods emporium in Chicago on State Street. It didn't take long before Selfridge went from a stockroom boy to assistant manager of retail at Marshall Field's State Street store.

Selfridge had ideas—and morals. Shoppers, he demanded, should never be lied to or presented with goods that were misrepresented. This apparently was a bold declaration in a business where cut-throat selling meant fibbing a little, if not a lot. Appearances meant everything and he insisted those who worked the floor be impec-cably dressed and meticulously groomed. He himself had a shave and trim of his mustache every morning before slipping into one of his dozen or so finely pressed suits with silk lapels. Besides per-sonal appearances, the look of the store needed an upgrade too. Selfridge installed more electrical lighting in the dimly lit corners and display windows where goods could be seen from the streets even at night. He hired a switchboard operator to handle the inter-nal phone calls between departments, and in his most boldly ambi-tious plan yet, he asked Field to open a restaurant inside the store. Field was hesitant at first. "This is a dry-goods store," he insisted. "We don't feed people here." But Selfridge convinced him that a restaurant would keep people in the store longer, and in 1890 the first "tearoom" opened at Marshall Field's on the third floor next to the fur department.

By the turn of the twentieth century, Field was ready to retire. Selfridge never doubted he would at least be in the running to head the company, but Field picked a man named John G. Shedd to be his successor, not Selfridge. Field apparently thought Shedd was a better money man and there was more to the business of run-ning a retail store than just sprucing up the displays. Disappoint-ed, Selfridge started thinking about leaving Field's and opening a store of his own. In May of 1903, he got that chance.

David Mayer of a competitor's store, Schlesinger and Mayer's, just down the street from Field's, had been negotiating a deal to merge with another department store, Carson's. He intended to rebrand the two into a dream-shopping emporium he had envi-

sioned nearly three decades before with partner Leopold Schlesinger, a wealthy German immigrant. But Carson's dragged on
the merger, and Mayer decided to sell and release himself from
the debt. Schlesinger had already quit the business, so Selfridge
jumped in. The beautiful, multistory store Mayer built on State
and Madison would be his, and he immediately installed new ban-
ners on the block that read "H.G. Selfridge and Co."

It didn't last.

Selfridge grew increasingly frustrated with day-to-day operations and the staff. He felt they were not matching the expertise
and enthusiasm he had seen at the Field's store. So only months
after opening the newly branded Selfridge store, it was changed
again. Surprisingly, it was John Shedd, Field's hand-picked successor, who stepped in. Shedd had bumped into John T. Pirie, the
managing partner of the Carson Pirie Scott & Co. run mostly by
his son Samuel Carson Pirie. The elder Pirie was still looking for
a showcase shop after the deal with Mayer to share the building at
State and Madison fell through. Shedd knew Selfridge was looking to sell so he brought the two together. They negotiated a deal
to buy Selfridge out for the initial $5-million-dollar investment
and a $250,000 bonus. Since more parties were legally involved,
Selfridge demanded another $150,000 to shore up loose ends. The
store on State Street would be Carson's exclusively.

An interesting anecdote to Selfridge's time in Chicago serves
as a testament to his commitment to please the public. One day a
young lady entered his Field's office asking for credit so she could
buy petticoats and lace frills for an upcoming dancing engagement. Broke and seemingly alone, Selfridge granted the young
lady's request. It's unclear whether Selfridge asked for her name
or knew who visited him that day, but Isadora Duncan never forgot his kind gesture.

In the weeks that followed the sale of the State Street store
to Carson's, Selfridge was bored and restless. He was after all a
career merchant and his brief stint as a department store owner,
while disappointing, just made the prospects more appealing. He
turned his attentions to London. The British were shopping snobs,
he was told, but Selfridge was going to change that. As the story

goes, while visiting one high-end London retailer, Selfridge was approached by a sales associate who asked him what he was intending to purchase. "I'm just looking," Selfridge replied. To that, the associate gave him a sneer and told him curtly to stop.

Selfridge claims he went back to Field to propose the idea of an Americanized store in London. If this was true, Field passed. Selfridge carried on. He looked for locations and found property on Oxford Street near Duke Street in the West End. Along with a wealthy businessman and English banker named Samuel Waring and Chicago architect Daniel Burnham, who designed Field's on State Street, he financed excavation on the new building and construction began in 1907. Selfridge originally wanted a large central tower, but height restrictions forbade it. Instead the five-story building would feature a showcase rooftop terrace on top.

On March 15, 1909, on a chilly and rainy London morning, Selfridges's department store opened its doors. While the crowds were large, the sales were not. Londoners just didn't get it. They walked and gawked and waited for someone to show them around. Selfridge began incorporating all his tools from the Field's days. A bargain basement was opened, and various specialized departments became popular, including a book section and a pet area carrying a selection of adorable puppies for sale.

Publicity was his game, so he seized on moments to arouse public awareness. When King Edward VII died suddenly, Selfridge draped the store's facade with black crepe. For the coronation of King George V and Queen Mary, he invited the young children of the Duke of Teck to safely view the procession from the store's high balcony. When the king's coach passed, the royal couple looked up and smiled at the children who were waving from above.

For all his success as a businessman, his reputation as a ladies' man also preceded him. His penchant for beautiful dancers is said to have led to numerous affairs while married. Even the name Isadora Duncan is rumored among them. Whether they ever had a physical romance is unclear; it is noted that Selfridge helped pay for Isadora to travel back to London during one of her tumultuous trips to New York. Mary Desti had asked Selfridge, who was also in New York and heading back to London, to pay Isadora's one-way ticket on the same steamer. During the trip, Isadora fell and broke her hip. Ordered to stay off her feet, Selfridge arranged for Isadora to use his private cabin for the rest of the voyage.

A decade before Selfridges became a staple of London's West End district, American theater manager Charles Frohman had leased the Duke of York's Theatre on St. Martin's Lane, and it quickly become one of the most successful playhouses in London. Frohman desperately wanted to showcase American plays overseas. Having a theater of his own was a good start. He decorated the lobby walls with pictures of current American stars he had personally developed, including his most-prized actress Maude Adams, who was to help propel both their careers. Soon they would team up for Frohman's most successful and famous production yet: a little play Frohman really liked, originally titled *The Great White Father*, soon to be changed to the simpler and more whimsical *Peter Pan*.

James M. Barrie, the English writer who created the play, sought out Frohman and together they made theater magic, their lives forever entwined by a boy who never grows up. That's where Selfridge, the self-made department store guru, reenters the picture. One day, a young lady walked into his department store, and Selfridge was smitten. Like Isadora Duncan, she was a dancer and he immediately doted on her, sending flowers and wine daily to the lavish London apartment Selfridge graciously leased for her.

The young lady was French-born Gaby Deslys, a dancer, singer, and aspiring actress. She found Selfridge's generosity and sentimentality charming. She also liked his money. With Selfridge's approval, Deslys racked up massive bills at Selfridges department store, which he gladly paid. At will, she purchased long expensive gowns and pearls and diamond necklaces and hats, lots of hats— that would become her trademark. Thanks to Selfridge, Deslys created a persona that led to her dancing getting noticed and a radiance that, in turn, attracted many influential men. One was James Barrie. After seeing her perform, like Selfridge, Barrie was also enthralled. Although not physical in nature, their relationship blossomed into a partnership. Deslys was thrilled to be working with the famous novelist and Barrie began to write plays for her.

5

Come to the theater prepared to fly

⟨⟨∅⟩⟩ Maude Adams was one of Frohman's handpicked projects, and at the age of twenty-five, already a seasoned actress. Ever since childhood her mother, Annie, another actress, had put little Maude in as many productions as she could. Since most melodramas had children in them, there were always parts to play. Child actors literally grew up on the stage, and theater producers like Frohman had a big influence on whether they became successful. Adams was one he carefully "manufactured," as one writer put it. But at that point she was still yet to be a star.

Then on September 27, 1897, Adams appeared as the lead in Barrie's play *The Little Minister* at the Empire Theatre in New York. At the end, there were so many curtain calls for the young actress that co-star Robert Edeson jokingly complained his arm grew tired escorting her back to the stage. The show ran for three hundred performances mostly to "standing room only" audiences and grossed $370,000, a new record for a Broadway show. On the last night of the run, Barrie sent a cablegram to Adams. "Thank you, thank you all for your brilliant achievement," he wrote.

After the success of *The Little Minister*, Charles Frohman and Barrie had several more hits together, mostly forgettable plays in themselves, but always with Maude Adams as the star. Then Adams disappeared. Many thought she had retired at the peak of her career, but she was actually in France recovering at a quiet convent from an appendicitis operation. In the meantime, Frohman was looking for more from Barrie, and Barrie assured him he would come up with something new. Then one night at the Garrick Club in London, Barrie seemed nervous. "What's the matter?" Frohman asked. "Simply this," Barrie replied, "you know I have an agreement to deliver a manuscript of a play? Well, I have it all right and I am anxious to see it on stage."

When Frohman read the script for what would become *Peter Pan, or the Boy Who Wouldn't Grow Up* he shook with delight. Frohman told Barrie that he would produce a version of *Peter* in London and in New York. He also had another suggestion: Frohman wanted Maude Adams to star as Peter. Barrie agreed, but she wasn't available until the next summer and Frohman was impatient. He wanted to get started right away. He instructed his London West End Company to begin preparations immediately. Adams would be ready when the production opened in America. Englanders would get *Peter Pan* first and Frohman set out to find an actress to play the part.

Considering what we know about the play today, it seems odd that there were some acquaintances of Barrie who were less than enthusiastic about its success. This is what they knew: Barrie had written a play quickly—in four months—and based it on a character named Peter in his book *The Little White Bird*. Peter was a baby boy who had wings and could fly. The strange tale involved a talking old crow and fairies who inhabit Kensington Square at night, a place Barrie knew well since he had a home near there. What adventures awaited this relatively unknown character named Peter Pan? That could only be imagined. Barrie kept it all a secret.

When he finished, Barrie read the script to theater manager and friend Herbert Beerbohm Tree, who then went to Frohman with bad news. "Barrie has gone out of his mind," Beerbohm Tree told Frohman. "He just read me his play and I'm sorry to say but you ought to know, I have tested myself upon hearing it, but Barrie must be mad." What exactly Beerbohm Tree disliked about the play is unclear. One thing that was clear, however, was Frohman's reaction. He dismissed Beerbohm Tree's warning outright and

The Little Minister. The Library of Congress, part of the theatrical poster division, Strobridge & Co. Lithograph [1897].

Maude Adams as Peter Pan. Otto Sarony Co., public domain [1904-1905].

preceded with planning. The only thing Frohman didn't like was Barrie's suggested title, *The Great White Father*, so it was changed.

Barrie had his own reservations. Perhaps being modest, he told Frohman, "It will not be a commercial success, but it is a dream-child of mine." Again, for Frohman, it fell on deaf ears. He loved the characters and the challenge of staging a show that included a place called Neverland, crocodiles, a pirate with an iron hook for a hand, and flying children.

Rehearsals for the London show included one day when the actors were told they should "come to the theater prepared to fly." Frohman had hired a man named George Kirby of the Flying Ballet Company to improve the harnesses that were used for some of the musicals Frohman produced. Frohman told Kirby to devise a system that was less visible. Kirby did, although it was so bulky and complicated that some of the backstage hands complained that it was they who were doing all the work, not the actors.

It was Frohman's idea to have a female adult actress play Peter in a gender-reversing role. Only a woman, Frohman insisted, could pull off the innocence and childlike behavior needed to play a young boy. Barrie agreed. Plus, if Peter was played by a boy at real age, then for continuity's sake the other children's roles would have to be the same age too. Under English law, minors fourteen or younger could not be on stage after 9:00 P.M.

Nina Boucicault was the English-born actress Frohman picked to play Peter in London. She too was praised. *"Peter Pan* from beginning to end is a pure delight," wrote the *London Times*. The second London run would also be a big success, but it was different from the first. Boucicault was no longer in the lead role by her own choice. The first run had worn her out physically and by the end she was missing performances. This time Frohman put Cecilia Loftus in her place. With a soft, sweet face and thin wispy smile, Loftus had just turned thirty but looked much younger. Born into a family of dance-hall entertainers, she was chosen to play Peter in early November just weeks before rehearsals.

Around the same time in America, on November 6, 1905, *Peter Pan* starring Maude Adams opened as scheduled in New York at Frohman's Empire Theatre. Even Mark Twain, at age seventy, chimed in. He penned a letter and addressed it directly to Adams herself. "It is my belief that *Peter Pan* is a great and refining and uplifting benefaction to this sordid tale and money mad-age, and the next best play on the boards is a long way behind it as long as you play Peter," he wrote.

Before the second run of *Peter Pan* opened in London, Frohman sent Loftus to meet Adams at the opening in America. Then Loftus went back to London to interview with Barrie. "I found him just as timid as I was," she recalled.

Cecilia Loftus was an unusual choice. She had more experience as a singer than an actress, and Peter, in the play, does not sing. In one of her few stage roles, however, she played Ophelia in Shakespeare's *Hamlet*. Frohman it seems had to make a quick decision and Loftus was it. Today, she is known for being the "second" Peter Pan and not much else.

Next to play Peter was an actress named Pauline Chase. Chase was something different altogether. First, at age twenty, she was the youngest to play Peter. She was also the first to have been with the show from the very first production in London. Barrie liked Chase. He later said of her performance: "There are only two possible ways to play Peter Pan. Either he must be a whimsical, fairy creature like Nina Boucicault, or he must be a lovable tomboy like Pauline Chase."

Born in Washington, D.C., in 1885, Chase made her stage debut at the age of thirteen. Mostly secondary and unheralded roles followed until 1903 when she was cast in *The Liberty Belles* and wowed audiences in a dance scene wearing pink pajamas. When the story broke that she chose the pajamas and picked out the color herself, she became known as "the Pink-Pajama Girl."

Charles Frohman took notice and hired her for a London production of *The School Girl*. When the original *Peter Pan* opened in London, she was cast as one of the Lost Boys. Frohman had the director add a scene where Chase wore pajamas and danced with her legs in two pillows cases like she had done for *Belles*. In the second run, with Cecilia Loftus as Peter, Chase became her understudy. When the company toured Scotland, she was alerted: Loftus had gotten ill, and Chase was up. As she began preparations for that night's performance in Edinburgh, another company member approached her. "Would you feel more nervous if Mr. Barrie chanced to be sitting in the front row?"

"Good heavens," Chase replied, "if Mr. Barrie should be in the front row I think I would faint with fright."

They were only kidding. Barrie was still in London, nearly four hundred miles away and couldn't possibly make the show that night. But Frohman and Barrie would eventually have a say in the matter. At a show in Liverpool, Chase subbed for Loftus again. This time both men were there. Before the performance Frohman came to see Chase backstage. Frohman and Barrie would be leaving before the show ended to catch a train back to London, and she would receive a note on paper after the performance. If there was an X on it, Frohman informed her, she would be offered the lead role of Peter in the following season's production.

After the second act, Chase got the note.

It had an X on it.

Throughout her run as Peter Pan, Chase's personal life would get just as much attention as her professional one. Her relationships with men, including one with a popular British aviator named Claude Grahame-White, made headline news. "I have no time to waste on duffers," she once told a reporter, "with no position or money." Fortunately, Grahame-White had both.

Chase's relationship with Grahame-White would end but not without playing out scandalously in the papers. Chase had claimed Grahame-White proposed to her while he was in America, and she had accepted. "Yes. I'm very happy," she told the *New York Herald*. "We will be married in the spring in London." Her alleged fiancé, however, had no such desires. "Grahame-White owes allegiance to no woman," his manager angrily proclaimed.

Then on December 18, 1910, Grahame-White was badly injured attempting a flight from England to the European mainland while chasing a $20,000 prize. As he lay in a hospital bed, his thoughts turned to other fellow flyers, daredevils like himself, who were killed in such stunts. He was lucky for now, but for how long? He had a change of heart: he decided the profession was too danger-

Pauline Chase with pipes as Peter Pan. From the Bruce K. Hanson collection, courtesy of Bruce K. Hanson.

ous. Henceforth, he would stay in the aviation business but stay mostly out of airplanes. Of course, there went the fame and riches.

While sympathetic, Chase soon realized she had no future with Grahame-White. When a reporter asked what broke off their relationship, she answered: "After knowing him well I concluded that he could not compensate me from my retirement from the stage." Then they asked if she would ever get married. "I have had dozens of proposals and turned them all down," she said defiantly. "There is a small chance of my becoming Mrs. Anybody. Please, don't say that I am engaged to anyone else."

At the time, Chase was experiencing the joy and stardom that came with playing Barrie's most popular character. Children from all over the world wrote her letters as if she were the real Peter Pan. But it wasn't just children that admired her work. Unlike her predecessors, Chase's beauty shone through Peter's childlike playfulness. Even the *Chicago Tribune* sarcastically criticized her for being "distractingly pretty." After the show, male attendees wanted to meet her. One night backstage, after another standing ovation and several curtain calls, there was a knock on the dressing room door. Barrie had brought back a friend for her to meet. He was wearing a naval uniform, and she immediately recognized him from the papers—it was the famed British explorer Captain Robert Scott.

6

I glowed rather foolishly

⁓ Like many English folk heroes, Captain Robert Falcon Scott lived a life shaped by his ancestors, specifically his grandfather, also named Robert, who was a purser in the Royal Navy. Known as "Con" to the family, Scott was a good student and destined to become an engineer or scientist as other boys with good educations usually did. Instead, his father kept the military in the family and sent Con to a naval training school. There Scott studied aboard a stationary ship, the *Britannica,* as the Royal Navy groomed new officers. At age fifteen, he went to sea.

In 1899, at the age of twenty-nine, Scott wanted more, a personal test, to keep current with the naval standards expected of an officer. So he applied for and received a special command mission. He would lead an expedition to Antarctica. "The expedition commanded by Commander Scott has been the most successful that ever ventured into Polar Regions, north or south," the *London Times* declared. When it was over, Scott was hailed a hero. Scott had kept a meticulous journal so the idea of writing a book, published a year after their return, was hatched while still at sea.

The book was a solid seller and although Scott didn't make a fortune, it was still considerably more than he made as a naval captain. It wasn't however without its controversies. The *Daily Mail* had misconstrued a passage where Scott may have questioned the courage of his third officer, Ernest Shackleton. At one point, Shackleton had gotten ill and Scott wrote that he rode on the sledge. The *Mail* interpreted the passage to mean that Shackleton slowed down the rest of the crew by adding the extra weight to the sledge. Scott rebuked the remarks, even as written, claiming Shackleton "was extremely ill, and caused us great anxiety," but added that "he displayed the [most] extraordinary pluck and endurance, and managed to struggle on beside the sledge without adding his weight to our burden." Shackleton seemed to take no offense and praised the book as "beautifully got up and splendidly written."

Shackleton as it turned out would be the first of the *Discovery* crew members to go back to the ice, this time with the goal to be the first man to reach the South Pole. If Scott himself had his eyes on the pole, he kept mostly quiet about it. He was a best-selling author and, as best-selling authors often do, hung out in literary circles and met some of the famous writers of the day.

One was A. E. W. Mason.

Like Scott, Alfred, as he was called, was a man of adventure. Throughout his life he was a mountaineer, a politician, an actor, a cricket player, and even a spy on behalf of British intelligence in the First World War. First and foremost, though, in 1905, he was a prolific novelist who had written dozens of popular books including *The Four Feathers,* an adventure novel set against the backdrop of the Mahdist War. Mason knew Scott even before the *Discovery* mission, and now that Scott had added "author" to his list of accomplishments, Mason introduced him to another writer friend: J. M. Barrie. It was a friendship that began simply but would significantly send Scott into different directions of his life. "If Barrie liked to be in the company of explorers," Barrie's longtime secretary wrote, *"they* felt a natural sympathy with him."

Barrie confessed to Scott that he "fell into and raced" through his book and found it "intoxicating." He also told his new friend that he must see his play about a magical little boy named Peter. It had just opened for a new season in London and starred a young actress named Pauline Chase. They should meet, Barrie insisted.

What transpired between Scott and Chase is unclear. Their

Ernest Henry Shackleton and Captain Robert Falcon Scott. National Library of New Zealand, public domain [1902].

courtship, if there was one of any significance, was told through others. "He took her out for supper several times," Scott biographer Elspeth Huxley claims. "No more came of that." Another biographer goes a bit further, putting Chase at parties with Scott or taking long romantic walks with him in Barrie's gardens. Regardless of their status as a couple, one thing is clear: Scott's affections for Pauline Chase ended when he found someone else. Barrie knew a certain London sculptor named Katheen Bruce, and during a luncheon party thrown by a mutual friend, he introduced Scott to her.

Kathleen recognized Scott as others did, as the debonair *Discovery* captain who had become "intrusively popular" upon his return. That was three years earlier. Now he was at her side. "I glowed rather foolishly and suddenly," she wrote. Within months, they would be engaged.

Did Barrie purposely intervene? We don't know for sure. After seeing *Peter Pan,* Scott had expressed a desire to find a woman to marry and Barrie may have thought Kathleen was a better match than Pauline Chase. More telling was Barrie's reaction to their engagement, which he found out secondhand. Barrie was disappointed that Scott had not personally told him first. Kathleen felt bad for Barrie. She immediately wrote Scott: "We must not hurt so sensitive and dear a person. Please write [to him] *quite* by return of post...as nice a letter you can think of." The rift was smoothed over, and soon Barrie was letting others in on the news, including Pauline. He penned a letter to her: "Capt. Scott wrote to me and told me he is to be married to Kathleen Bruce, so there."

Shortly after Scott proposed, Kathleen told Isadora Duncan the exciting news. Isadora was happy for her friend but had exciting news of her own. She was going back to America. The great agent Charles Frohman had booked her as "The Rage of London," and insisted she come dance on his stages. Before she left, Isadora saw old friends and celebrated Kathleen's engagement. Two years later, after Isadora had completed several subsequent tours of North America, Mrs. Kathleen Scott had more news: first, she was pregnant, and, second, her husband was going back to Antarctica.

7

This is not her audience

⟋⟋ Charles Frohman had a good reputation with British imports, especially actresses, including Mrs. Pat, who had jump-started Isadora's career after a chance meeting in London's Kensington Square. Mrs. Pat and Frohman butted heads, mostly over artistic control, a creative line that many of his American actresses did not cross. Mrs. Pat was different. She fought for her rights as a performer and would not back down. She even refused to appear as Eliza Doolittle in George Bernard Shaw's *Pygmalion* until someone other than Richard Loraine played Professor Higgins. The true protagonist of *Pygmalion* was Eliza, not the professor, Mrs. Pat protested, and Loraine was too popular an actor to share the billing. In the end, a character-actor-turned-theater-manager, Sir Herbert Beerbohm Tree, described as "old fashioned," took the role opposite Mrs. Pat.

Now in America at the request of New York's most influential theater impresario, she fought over a particular scene in a German play being translated by Edith Wharton, an American writer who would become best known for her novels on the Gilded Age. The play was known in English as *The Joy of Living* and in question was the lead character of Countess Beata, played by Mrs. Pat. The premise went like this: Fifteen years before the play begins, Beata had ended an affair with Richard a close friend of her politi-

MRS. PATRICK CAMPBELL.
IN "THE NOTORIOUS MRS. EBBSMITH"

Mrs Pat Campbell. New York Public Library, from the Billy Rose Theater Division [1895].

cally connected husband Michael. Now salacious letters of their liaison have fallen into the wrong hands, and Michael could see a dangerous scandal brewing. Richard told Beata he would end his own life to save his friend and former lover. But sensing his quest to live, Beata took her own life instead by giving a speech at an official dinner, toasting to "a long life" and drinking a glass of wine mixed with a fatal heart medicine. She walks out of the room to die.

The irony of it all was lost, claimed Wharton, if the audience doesn't know Beata mixed the brew herself. Mrs. Pat agreed. Frohman did not. He was looking for an element of surprise and liked the idea of the audience guessing to the end. Frohman suggested a compromise by cutting a confrontation scene between Beata, Michael, and Richard. Mrs. Pat refused and Frohman left the production. Before he exited the theater, however, Mrs. Pat came downstage to engage him.

"Always remember, Mr. Frohman," she told him, "that I am an artist."

"Madam," Frohman countered, "I will keep your secret."

A snarky retort like that wasn't Frohman's style and Mrs. Pat thought she had won the debate. She carried on as producer, and the play opened just a few days past schedule.

Isadora Duncan never held that kind of resentment toward Frohman, but her time in America with the impresario was considerably less successful than Mrs. Pat's. Frohman managed many theaters in New York, but in London he had control of one, the Duke of York's. Isadora danced for him there, and Frohman signed her to a new American tour. She agreed to his offer, but more as a necessity than a choice. "I was already famous in Europe," she explained. "But as far as finances went, I was not much richer than before." Frohman heralded her American visit as "The Rage of London" and billed her thusly: "She will be the first example of a single artist devoting her whole evening to dancing, unrelieved by song, skit, or recitation."

For three weeks, Isadora would occupy the Criterion Theatre on 43rd Street. There was no narration or small talk, just an orchestra playing Beethoven's Seventh Symphony and Isadora dancing.

"She moves through the air as though it were the finer ether; the impression, though the eyes do see, is that she is as incorporeal as the sylphs, as fairy-footed as the elves," wrote Henry Taylor Parker of the *Boston Evening Transcript* and whose pseudonym was his acronym, HTP.

While describing the performance was easy, HTP had a hard time classifying Isadora's style. "It is fairest and clearest to name it Miss Duncan's dancing and leave it at that."

The first night started awkwardly. The orchestra played the wrong piece twice. Isadora stuck to her pose and was "immobile," the papers noted, until the music started up again and "she set them right."

Isadora noticed something wasn't right. American theatergoers, while polite, just weren't getting into it. And here's why: The previous year in 1907, *Ziegfeld Follies,* a successful French-inspired cabaret show opened on Broadway to rave reviews and packed audiences. The program was filled with rousing music, comedy skits, a chorus of dancing girls, and finely choreographed scenes. This was the kind of high-stepping, high-flying entertainment that was popular on Broadway at the time, not a two-hour dance "solo" without any words.

The *New York Telegraph* was kind enough to give her this consideration at least: "There are many in New York who knew her as the clever artist when she lived here many years ago, and of those many were present." The papers also played up her role as the hero of the Windsor Hotel fire. But in addition to the audience's indifference, something else was visibly wrong.

Isadora did not look well.

It was the middle of August and the heat was unbearable. The stifling humidity broke her spirit and wore her down. Isadora cut her performances from seven days a week to four and added more numbers this time to the music of Chopin. It seemed to help her confidence.

Frohman of course was watching it all from the wings. He was supportive but worried. Had he misjudged how "The Rage of London" would play in America? Others would let him know. An old friend William Harris was one. While he didn't speak to Frohman

Walter Damrosch. The Library of Congress, part of the prints and photographs division.

directly, a reporter for *Variety* overheard his conversation with a companion.

"Who handed such a lemon to Frohman?" Harris asked.

Harris was certainly someone who would know. A successful theater producer like Frohman, Harris was a onetime child actor who found his calling managing plays rather than appearing in them. He laid his foundation of theaters in Boston and owned a share of houses in New York and Chicago. He and Frohman had brokered deals together.

Harris's snipe about Isadora likely didn't faze Frohman. He had more weighty matters to attend. First was Isadora herself: she was threatening to quit. Frohman engaged her with honesty. "America does not understand your art," he said. "It would be better for you to go back to Europe." But the choice was hers.

Isadora was ready to break her six-month contract with Frohman and return to Europe when she met an American sculptor named George Grey Barnard, who begged her not to leave. Barnard attended many of Isadora's performances and often brought his artists friends with him. He would bring them backstage to meet her. Barnard was Isadora's western version of Rodin and, at only fourteen years her senior, much younger. She desired him. However, Barnard kept his distance and devotion to his wife. He "counseled me to stay in America," Isadora wrote, "and I'm glad I listened."

Another person who offered positive support was Mary Fanton Roberts, the editor of the arts magazine *The Touchstone*. One night, Roberts sought out Isadora backstage for an interview. Isadora's brother Augustin stopped Roberts at the door. Isadora was unhappy, he told her, and thinking about leaving. Roberts said angrily, "She must not do that! This is not her audience! She should have never danced in this theater."

Soon enough, Barnard introduced her to a composer named William Damrosch, a German-born American national and the conductor of the New York Symphony. Damrosch had seen Isadora perform and, as a musician, had been impressed. "I have never felt the real 'Joy of Life' in an almost primitive innocence and glory as her dance," he later wrote.

Damrosch was one of the world's top conductors at age forty-six, specializing in Wagner and working with just about every theater impresario in New York from Oscar Hammerstein I to Charles Frohman. Born into a musical family, Damrosch's father Leopold was a celebrated concert pianist who had the honor of playing with some of Europe's foremost piano maestros including the Russian Anton Rubenstein, who came to New York in 1872 and played a week of concerts at the Metropolitan Opera House. As a resident musician, Leopold was chosen to participate in a piano trio with Rubenstein and the Polish-born Henryk Wieniawski.

The New York concerts by Rubenstein and other well-known European virtuoso pianists were so popular that tours of eastern and Midwest cities were arranged. These lasted months and included stops in Terra Haute, Indiana, and Peoria, Illinois, smaller cities that usually weren't privy to such an honor. The local Peoria paper said of Rubenstein's performance, "We have never heard the likes of this before."

Walter Damrosch was just ten when Rubenstein came to America. He remembered the pianist giving an impromptu performance in his family's living room: "I sat google-eyed behind him, watching him do incredible things. I was beside myself with excitement as his hand made this terrific jump over the keys again and again hitting the high notes with the precision of a marksman hitting the target in the center with every shot."

After visiting her studio, Damrosch asked Isadora to come dance for him at the Met among other places. Isadora needed no convincing. If she was to be successful in America, Damrosch was her last chance. This time it worked. In the concert halls packed with music-appreciative audiences and given Damrosch's reputation, Isadora thrived. From New York, they went on a successful tour to Philadelphia, Washington, D.C., Chicago, and St Louis. When the tour ended, Isadora returned to Europe both happy and considerably richer. "If it had not been for the pulling at my heartstrings to see my baby [Deirdre]…I would have never left America."

Deirdre was Isadora's infant daughter from a man named Edward Henry Gordon Craig, a stage designer whom she met after the sojourn in Greece. Craig, the son of the great British actress

Ellen Terry, was five years younger than Isadora. He was also married and had several children with several different women. These included an Italian violinist named Elena Meo, who when Craig met Isadora, was pregnant with Craig's child, their third together. Isadora didn't seem to mind. "This was not a young man making love to a girl. This was the meeting of twin souls," she wrote transfixed. On September 24, 1906, Isadora bore a child after a long and painful labor. She named her Deirdre, after the mythical Irish heroine, Deirdre of the Sorrows.

After returning home to Deirdre, Isadora would look back at her association with Frohman this way: "Charles Frohman was a great manager," she wrote, "but he failed to realize my art was not of a theatrical venture. It could only appeal to a certain restricted public. The few people who wandered into the theater on those torrid nights when the temperature was ninety degrees were bewildered and, most of them, not pleased with what they saw. The result as you might have expected, was a flat failure."

8

A pleasant and cultivated taste

For Frohman it was a rare miss. Still, there were no hard feelings. *Peter Pan,* his latest triumph, was an annual tradition, and along the way there would be a slew of memorable shows and performers, dozens of who would personally extend a debt of gratitude to the man who started or outright made their careers. "He loved his schemes," Barrie would write about his friend, referring to his people. "They were a succession of many-colored romances to him." Frohman's famous, third-floor office in the Empire Theatre was lined with pictures of his "stars" and in the middle, a flattop desk, where "much of the American theater passed," one observer noted. He practically lived there.

When he was in London, Frohman stayed at the luxurious Savoy Hotel. The Savoy was as modern as it got back then, and Frohman fit right in. Of the 268 opulent rooms, 67 had private marble bathrooms and all were "plumbed" with running hot water available for a bath both day and night. "For luxury, comfort, and safety, the accommodations in the Savoy Hotel far transcend anything yet attempted elsewhere," read the *Dublin Freeman Journal* in 1889, the hotel's first year. Every day, without fail, Frohman was a regular at the hotel's posh Savoy Grill, where the servers set the same table for him precisely at noon. This is where he met George Kessler.

Kessler was the man who had challenged Oscar Hammerstein to a fistfight when Hammerstein booed and hissed a production Kessler supported. Their confrontation, which put Hammerstein in jail for a time, subsequently led to the opening of Hammerstein's groundbreaking Olympia Theatre complex.

Known as the "the Champagne King," Kessler was a wealthy, dark-bearded, wine importer from America who lived extravagantly and wasn't shy about letting it show. As an agent for Moët & Chandon, the popular champagne makers of the day, Kessler spent a good portion of his time in Europe. "He is a fine type of New York's self-made man," an English journal pointed out, "...with a natural affinity for beauty, and a pleasant and cultivated taste."

His fortune came from parties and the people who planned, hosted, and attended them. Kessler also owned his own label of champagne called the White Star that Moët sponsored. Often, he would throw fancy parties himself just to drum up sales and cavort with friends and business associates. Kessler knew how to please old clients and court new ones. He gave out free bottles like candy, always pleasing both potential buyers and suppliers. He never missed an opportunity to promote his product.

Like Frohman, Kessler was a regular at the Savoy Hotel, but for a vastly different reason: he was there to sell wine. He also hosted legendary parties. One party Kessler threw in 1905 for King Edward VII defies imagination. It is still remembered today as one of the most lavish and bizarre affairs ever. A Venetian-style gondola, trumpeter swans, white doves, even a baby elephant on loan from the London Zoo all graced the night's festivities. Kessler and his planners had turned the hotel's courtyard into a Venetian scene, complete with a three-foot-deep canal. The twenty-four invited guests boarded the gondola and floated down the canal from the hotel lobby to their seats. After dinner a five-foot birthday cake arrived on the back of the elephant as handlers lumbered the animal across an arched bridge.

There is no record of Charles Frohman attending the "Gondola Party" as it would later be called. Likely, he did not. Frohman traveled constantly between America and London, and his time in London consisted of meetings, theater rehearsals, and the inevitable lunch at the Savoy Grill. Whether Frohman or Kessler conversed at some length is not known, but they both knew each other. Based on their status and wealth, they would have crossed the Atlantic together on the best ships and in the best accommodations.

For both Frohman and Kessler traveling was time-consuming, but necessary. Since there was no alternative, making the best of an Atlantic crossing—typically five days or more—usually involved drinking. Since it was his wine the passengers were consuming, Kessler certainly didn't mind. In fact, he often threw the parties himself. Frohman conversely would be more introspective, always thinking ahead, writing letters and using the ship's telegraph operator to send messages.

Then on April 15, 1912, an event took place that gave frequent ocean travelers like Frohman and Kessler pause. The largest steamer ever built, on its maiden voyage from Southampton to New York, had struck an iceberg and sank in the icy waters of the Atlantic killing 1,500 passengers and crew. For Frohman, the *Titanic* disaster was also personal. One of victims was another theater producer, Henry B. Harris, the son of William Harris, who had brokered a deal with Frohman that led to the opening of the Empire Theatre. Frohman knew Henry well. They had done business together in New York, and many of Henry's productions on Broadway competed with Frohman's. The two had recently haggled over a star-in-the making Ann Murdock.

Harris was working on another production and returning to New York with his wife, Renee, an actress, who survived the sinking. They were to be joined by an actor named Edgar Selwyn, who at the last minute decided to stay behind in London. Selwyn became a part of the "Just Missed It Club"—an actual group of people, hundreds in fact, who claimed their fate was decided by extraordinary, oftentimes bizarre, circumstances. In Selwyn's case it was an English author he admired, Arnold Bennet, who promised Selwyn an early draft of his new novel if he just waited. He did. Henry B. Harris had no such luck. He became "passenger 36973, Cabin C-83, *deceased.*" Like many others who perished that night, his body was never recovered.

Frohman had assumed another acquaintance was on board the

Henry B. Harris. New York Public Library, from the Billy Rose Theater Division [1901].

Titanic as well: a man named Charles Klein. Klein worked as a script editor for Frohman in the early days of the Empire Theatre and was a mutual friend of Harris. Frohman had recently produced plays that Klein had written. When Frohman heard about the *Titanic* sinking, he knew Klein had booked passage on the maiden voyage because Frohman was expecting him back in New York. What he didn't know, however, was that Klein had been delayed by a business meeting in London and never made it to the ship. Later, Klein would give his thoughts on Harris and the others who perished. "That's a terrible way to die," he said. "To know there is no way to escape and wait for death helplessly—it's horrible."

At first, the *Titanic* sinking was seen as a random and accidental tragedy, an act of fate, rather than poor judgment. That attitude would change. But in the years ahead, something more disturbing would concern the passengers and crews of these large ships crossing the open water.

The drumbeat of war was sounding.

9
Here is my millionaire

_____

Kathleen Scott was alone with her thoughts for about a month after her husband departed for Antarctica. The timing of Captain Scott's decision to return to the ice came just a day before their son Peter was born in September of 1909. Scott signed the papers and was given the green light by the Royal Geographic Society and the Admiralty to assemble a crew for a return to the Antarctic—this time to reach the South Pole. Kathleen was worried, but supportive of her husband. She always knew his determination and drive might one day take him away from her—far away, and perhaps for a long period of time. The crew was scheduled to depart in the summer of 1910, leaving Kathleen, Scott, and baby Peter only eight short months together. If everything proceeded as planned, Scott would return to them in two years.

The journey to goodbyes began that following summer in July, though the ship named *Terra Nova* did not leave New Zealand until the end of November. Shortly after Scott and the crew set off, Kathleen spent time with his family in Sydney waiting for a boat to take her back to England.

Kathleen's thoughts were also fixed on her friend Isadora Duncan. It had been a turbulent but eventful year for the dancer, and Kathleen had had little time to spend with her. So she changed plans and took a ship from Marseilles to Paris, hoping to find Isa-

Robert and Kathleen Scott. National Library of New Zealand, public domain [1910].

dora at her home near Rodin's studio. She was disappointed: Isadora had just left for New York. Nevertheless, Mrs. Scott was welcomed by Isadora's sister Elizabeth and Edward Craig who was there to visit his daughter Deirdre. Also, there was Isadora's new baby, a boy named Patrick. Although Craig could claim a string of children from several different women, Patrick was not one of them. Craig and Isadora had ended their relationship shortly after Deirdre was born and Isadora had found a new man to love—Paris Singer, a wealthy businessman, who was Patrick's father.

Singer and Isadora first met in Paris in 1909 at the Gaîté-Lyrique Theatre where Isadora was doing a series of performances, her first in the "City of Lights" since 1904. Isadora was still a draw despite the emergence of ballet, especially Russian ballet, which had recently become popular in the city. The Ballets Russes was in town and the theater's grand tiers were packed with actors and artists, like Rodin, who were all given special invitations. Isadora was there too. She loved what she saw, but the feelings weren't mutual. An accomplished Russian ballet dancer named Anna Pavlova was asked about Isadora. "You see," Pavlova said, "she never has to get up and dance on her toes, but I do." Socially, there was an even bigger disconnect. "She lives to dance," Pavlova added, "and I dance to live."

Isadora continued to perform sold-out shows to appreciative audiences. Her work, however, had changed a bit; it was becoming darker and more disturbing. "It is the eternal mystery of death in all its anguished simplicity," a writer for a French magazine imposed about her work. "I am only reporting the facts. I saw people weeping who were laughing when it started." It was in this environment, at this time in Isadora's life, that she found Paris Singer.

Named for the city he was born in, Paris was the second youngest child of Isaac Merritt Singer, a notorious philanderer who had fathered twenty-five children, only six of whom, including Paris, shared the same mother. Singer had the money to support them all, so he did. Paris's mother Isabella, of French descent, had married Isaac in New York when she was just twenty-one.

In 1875, when Paris was just seven, his father died leaving him a sizable income from investments that totaled $15,000 a week (over

a million dollars in today's money, at least). The elder Singer's fortune came from the mass manufacturing of a machine that was to
become the highly successful Singer Sewing Machine Company.
Paris was too young to handle such an accruement of wealth and
by his own admission became a ward of the British Court. He eventually went to Cambridge and studied science, medicine, and engineering. Like his father, Paris couldn't keep his hands off the ladies.
Before turning twenty he eloped with one of his mother's servants
–a marriage that was quickly annulled–and then went on to marry
an Australian woman with whom he fathered five children.

Educated, charitable, romantic, and handsome were the traits
Isadora found endearing when Singer presented himself to her one
day in the dressing room of the Gaîté-Lyrique Theatre. But something else was appealing as well. When the maid asked if she could
bring Mr. Singer in, Isadora recognized the name.

Here is my millionaire, she thought to herself.

"Let him enter!" she said excitedly.

Singer, like Edward Craig, was a married man, but at least he
was separated from his wife. His five children, four of them sons,
seemed to adore him. Singer told Isadora he was impressed with
her dancing school in Paris and wanted his own daughter Wina-
retta to join in. Isadora imagined all the wonderful things he could
do for her school.

Craig was mostly out of the picture at this point although they
would often see each other because of Deirdre. Like she did with
Craig, Isadora fell for Singer at first sight. They traveled and stayed
in elegant homes and villas in various countries. One palatial estate
was on the scenic Devonshire coast. Some years after his father's
death, Singer transformed it into an even grander vision, a replica
of the Palace of Versailles.

Isadora kept up a busy schedule. She traveled to Russia and Paris
and back to North America for a second tour in New York. She was
pregnant but tried to keep it hidden. By early December of 1909,
in her farewell concert at Carnegie Hall, it was hard to conceal.

"My dear Miss Duncan," a rather outspoken woman told her
backstage, "it's plainly visible from the front row."

Isadora Duncan and Paris Singer. The Library of Congress, part of the Genthe Collection [1916].

Knickerbocker Theater, far right on Broadway Street north from 38th. The Library of Congress, part of the prints and photographs division, American Studio N.Y. [1920].

Act III

⚬ "The choices we make every minute of every day can contribute to making someone's life a little bit better or worse even without intending to." *–Chikamso Efobi*

During the performance of a play titled *The Hyphen,* actor William H. Thompson was delivering a dramatic soliloquy when his words were suddenly interrupted.

No one in the audience was surprised.

The Hyphen by Justus Miles Forman had just opened at the Knickerbocker Theatre in New York and tensions were high. The "hyphen" in the title referred to the hyphen in the word "German-Americans." The play was about the conflict between the German-Americans who supported the alliance in the fight overseas and those who remained loyal to the Homeland.

It was April 12, 1915, and the war was on in Europe.

Toward the end of the first act of the play, Thompson, playing a German immigrant loyal to his adopted country, stands center stage and delivers a speech. In it he pleads for his fellow countrymen for "less meddling."

On this particular night, there was meddling.

A man seated in the front row took exception to the speech and began shouting his support for Germany, the Kaiser, and the war.

Thompson stopped briefly. He looked at the gentleman and continued with the speech emphasizing the words pointedly at the offender. Hisses filled the theater as the man was escorted down the aisle.

After he was gone, Thompson continued. But the disruptions would not end.

Later during another act, the play was halted again.

This time it was even more disturbing.

A loud bang, like a bomb going off, was heard coming from outside the theater's front doors.

1

An adorable
blonde doll

C✆Ꝺ On September 29, 1906, the curtains at the Gaiety Theatre in London's West End rose to a new production of an old
story, *Aladdin*. By rights, it was *Aladdin* by name only. The story
was revamped into a romp, a musical farce complete with magic
lamp and genie from the original, but not much else—except of
course that in the end love does conquer all. There was dancing
and songs and chorus girls and lavish costumes.

The Aladdin part that night was played by Lily Elsie in another
gender-reversal role. "Little Elsie," as she was known early in her
career, began as a child actor and appeared in many productions
that were staged almost always around Christmastime. She had
the title role of *Little Red Riding Hood* when she was just ten. By
the time she was in her teens she was touring with productions
of British musical troupes, popular at the time and known as Edwardian musical comedies, named after King Edward VII and the
era that began upon Queen Victoria's death in 1901 and continued until 1910.

Appropriately enough, the man who is known as the "Father
of Edwardian Musicals" was named George Edwardes, a theater
manager and producer, like Charles Frohman, who took over the
Gaiety Theatre in the late 1800s. Then known for its risqué burlesque numbers, Edwardes toned the Gaiety down a bit. He opened

shows that featured big musical numbers and lavish sets, but with less controversial chorus lines.

Lily Elsie was not Edwardes's initial choice to play the title role in *Aladdin.* That was English-born actress Gertie Millar, one of the most popular actresses in London at the time. Another child-actor-turned-successful-stage-actress, Millar rose to fame as the star of several long-running hits before *Aladdin.* Just before opening night, though, Millar's husband, Lionel Monckton, a well-known composer, fell ill. Millar stayed home to care for him. Edwardes while disappointed, understood and chose Elsie to begin the first run. Millar would join the production when she was ready.

The New Aladdin, as it was billed, opened to much anticipation. By the end of the first night, however, the excitement had subsided. The play received mostly poor reviews and the audience was said to be bored, especially during the second and final act when they were restless and talking amongst themselves. At the curtain call, the crowd politely stood and cheered the cast, but not much else.

It wasn't Elsie's fault, she did her best, and when Millar triumphantly returned and joined the cast, the play found its legs, so to speak, simply by star power alone.

However, before Millar gave *The New Aladdin* the boost that it sorely needed, there was a young actress in the show who grabbed the most applause from opening night. She appeared in just a few scenes, most notably one in which she is summoned by the genie after he rubs the lamp and wishes for the "Charms of Paris." From a basket of silk roses, she appears in a low-cut dress and high-buttoned boots. Later, emerging as a French maid in a bathing dress and discreet bra with each breast covered by a glittering starfish, she sings a song in a low, seductive voice: "At what do the men all stare," she sings, "when I take my *bains de mer* [bath]?" The house erupted in wild applause.

"Who is that girl?" they seemed to ask.

It was Gaby Deslys.

Born in Marseilles in 1881, Deslys was one of four siblings including two sisters. Gaby seemed to be the most outgoing of the three girls and her father Hippolyte, who ran a successful textile business, insisted she get a good education. He paid to send her to a prestigious convent school, but Deslys, while smart, was not a very good student. She wanted out of the books and onto the stage. With her mother Anna's blessing, Deslys enrolled in a conservatoire in Marseilles to learn to sing. She was flourishing until the family went into mourning. Her oldest sister, Aimee, who had just married, succumbed to tuberculosis. Deslys stepped away from classes to grieve. When she returned, she was behind on her schoolwork but still passed. Eventually she felt comfortable enough with her own singing voice to search for a job.

Finding work as an actress, however, proved to be more difficult than she imagined. Pretty girls like herself were all vying for spots in the local theaters, many with more stage experience than Deslys. Staying in Marseilles however was never in her plans. Bigger aspirations meant leaving home, which displeased her father, but it was not his decision to make. She was, after all, twenty-one.

She was going to Paris.

As Mrs. Pat did for Isadora Duncan, Deslys's big break came from another actor, George Grossmith, Jr., whose father was a well-known English stage comedian. As he did every weekend, after a Saturday performance at the Gaiety, Grossmith would catch a train to Paris to spend a quiet Sunday there before returning to London on Monday. During one weekend, he decided to catch a musical revue at the Olympia Theatre. He was looking for girls for Edwardes's productions. The revue *Au Music Hall* had just opened in May of 1905, and it was considered a hoot. A group of girls danced and sang, including Deslys. She appeared in several of the numbers, often alone, and always in her trademark feathered hats, short skirts, and high-buttoned boots. Grossmith took notice. When he returned to London, he met with Edwardes and discussed the upcoming production of *The New Aladdin*. They had been searching for a girl to play the part of the pretty French maid. Deslys spoke little English, he told Edwardes, but she didn't need to. She only needed to sing the bath song in her native French. It was a perfect match, Grossmith thought, and Edwardes agreed.

Grossmith was also in *The New Aladdin,* cast to play the genie. Long and lanky, he appeared in many productions with actor Edward Payne who was just as short as Grossmith was tall. Together they were a mismatched pair, similar to the popular comedy duos that would appear later in silent films like Laurel and Hardy and Abbot and Costello. Until Gertie Millar rejoined the cast of *The New Aladdin,* Grossmith and Payne were the stars of the show.

That is until everyone started talking about Gaby Deslys

The bit part in *The New Aladdin* paid the bills and got her noticed, but Deslys wanted more. She found promoting herself through looks and actions was the ticket to stardom. As for looks, there was nothing to change. "An adorable blonde doll," one admirer remarked upon meeting her for the first time. As for actions, Deslys stepped out and allowed herself to be seen. Night after night, she appeared on the arm of another handsome male suitor—no scandal, just talk. These were men who had influence and, equally important, money. One of them was the department store owner Harry Gordon Selfridge. He longed for her, pursued her, and eventually won her over with the lavish gifts he could provide from his store cases. While he was more than twenty years her senior, she graciously accepted his generosity. In turn, Deslys amassed a small fortune of fine jewels, furs, and elaborate hats.

When her stint in *The New Aladdin* ended, Deslys traveled with revues between Paris and London. When in London, she stayed across from Kensington Square in one of Selfridge's fully furnished homes. Her performances became more expressive and seductive. She wore short tutus and thin-strapped tops, some beaded, that barely covered what was underneath. It was noted how she had changed from her role in *The New Aladdin.* This was a more confident Deslys, and her singing, while not as refined as others, was low in tone and very seductive.

One night during a performance in Berlin, Kaiser Wilhelm's son the Crown Prince Wilhelm was in attendance. Afterward he went backstage to meet Deslys and asked that she accompany him and two friends to dinner. The prince, known as "Little Willie" to the press, was not shy about his obsession with sexy actresses. The European newspapers picked up on their budding romance and exploited it. The prince was madly in love with Deslys, they reported. Deslys made no comment. It would end but not before

Gaby Deslys. The Library of Congress, part of the prints and photographs division [1912].

the papers speculated that the Kaiser himself intervened by giving
Deslys three large black pearls if she would let "Little Willie" go.
She did.

Then came *A la Carte,* the show that nearly ended it all. After successful runs with touring revues in Germany, France, and America, Deslys's return to London was a sensation. She was up for anything, and *A la Carte* was that and more. Anyone who walked past
the Palace Theatre could hardly miss it. Large letters above the
marquee announced "She's Back" and a cutout image of Deslys
lying down with her hand on her chin was plastered above the
theater entrance door. Even before the show opened, the papers
ran pictures of the show's revealing costumes. By the time the curtain finally went up, Deslys and *A la Carte* had already created a
buzz. She was pleased, but not everyone shared her enthusiasm.
One night, the Bishop of Kensington went to see the show. In one
scene Deslys powders her leg straight up to her upper thigh, followed by a song-and-dance number in which Deslys navigates a
high staircase while gyrating her mid-section. To top it all off, Deslys gets swept up the stairs by a male actor while she wraps her
legs around his waist.

The audience loved it; the bishop did not.

The bishop immediately contacted the Lord Chamberlin's office
and complained that parts of the show were "grossly indecent."
In turn, the comptroller of the office, Sir Douglas Dawson, sent
a letter to the theater's manager: "If Public Morality be any further outraged at the Palace Theatre," he wrote, "the piece in question will be immediately forbidden and your license for plays will
be cancelled." Deslys was the target of their slinging arrows, but
the manager of the show, a man named Alfred Butts, defended
her. He called out the bishop for making a rash judgement of Deslys, the person, already labeling her immoral and not judging the
performance itself. Let the people decide, he implored, if she is
indecent or not. Deslys, herself, sent a letter defending her right
to do what other actors and actresses were doing on stages "the
whole world over." In this instance, the bishop was signaling her
out based on her reputation off the stage. Even those who saw the
show along with the bishop, wrote to the *Times* to support her. It

was pure "sexual emotion," one patron wrote describing Deslys's actions, not "corruption or vice."

Deslys would continue with the play even though the press was there to greet her after every performance. One night, there was an unexpected visitor. "Someone is here to see you," Butts explained discreetly from behind the dressing room door. She motioned for the maid to let them in.

"Gaby," Butts said to her, "I'd like you to meet an old friend old mine."

She recognized him right away.

It was James Barrie, the author of *Peter Pan.*

2

Into Thy hands, O Lord

CSD On April 29, 1912, in the dead of night, while Londoners were fast asleep, a statue of Peter Pan was erected on the grounds of Kensington Gardens. The man hired to create the fourteen-foot-tall bronze statue was famed British sculptor Sir George Frampton. James Barrie insisted it be installed in the cover of darkness. That way in the morning on the first day of May when strollers returned to the park the statue would appear there as if by magic. Frampton worked in secrecy so they could pull off the surprise.

This was eight years after *Peter Pan* first opened in London, and much had changed since then. In October of 1905, less than a year after the first performance of *Peter* at the Duke of York's Theatre and just a month before the play premiered in New York with Maude Adams, the West End was rocked by the news that its favorite son, Sir Henry Irving, was dead. Irving was the longstanding owner and manager of the Lyceum Theatre on Strand Street and since 1878 had presented an array of Shakespeare's finest plays, legendary not only for the words but for the two stars that read them: Irving himself and the formidable Ellen Terry, mother of Edward Gordon Craig and grandmother of Deirdre, Isadora Duncan's daughter by Craig.

Like Charles Frohman, Irving got his start humbly, born in 1838 to a working-class couple in a Somerset neighborhood. His father

Sir Henry Irving. Cleveland Museum of Art, public domain [1910].

owned a grocery store and traveled constantly to sell wares. Irving stayed mostly with an aunt but did well enough in school to get a job working for a law firm at the age of thirteen. Around this same time he saw *Hamlet;* it changed him. He sought an acting coach and soon found work at the Lyceum Theatre. Irving worked for years, mostly in secondary roles, until *The Bells* opened in November 1871 and ran for 151 performances. Irving played the lead role of the burgomaster, Mathias, who is haunted by guilt after killing a man for money on Christmas Eve. Only he and the audience can hear the sound of sleigh bells jingling and the appearance of the victim's ghostly face until it slowly drives Mathias insane. From the opening night performance, critics declared Irving a new star, and he quickly became one of Britain's leading actors. Anyone interested in theater made it a point to see the play.

When Irving took over the Lyceum in 1878, he was the most-talked-about actor in England and the Shakespeare plays he produced with Ellen Terry were big draws. Among his many admirers was his longtime personal assistant at the Lyceum, Bram Stoker, a budding writer who may have actually based his most popular character Dracula after Irving. "A tall old man, save for a long white mustache and clad in black from head to foot, without a single speck of color about him," is the way Stoker describes Count Dracula in his novel. Whether he was also describing Irving is debatable. Stoker also added, "...pointed ears and sharp teeth," so the comparisons likely ended there.

It was also Stoker who in 1905 began to sense that Irving at the age of sixty-seven was too ill to perform. After another revival of *The Bells* in Bradford, England, Stoker secretly packed up the scenery and sent it back to London. Stoker had hoped his friend would retire, but Irving went on stage one last time in Alfred Tennyson's *Becket,* uttering the final lines "Into Thy hands, O Lord, Into Thy Hands," before suffering a stroke and dying an hour later.

At the time of his death, Irving was no longer the owner of the Lyceum, and the London theater scene was transitioning. Instead of the classics, new productions were setting the stage for the new century. Frohman's *Peter Pan* was one. Irving's influence, however, was immense. Whether Irving and Frohman were adversaries or friends in London where they had competing theaters is unknown, but when Irving sent Stoker to the United States to scout locations for the Shakespeare tour, he gave Stoker this advice: "When you get to America just tell Frohman that I want to come under his management. He always understands. He is always fair."

In 1895, ten years before he died, Irving was knighted by Queen Victoria, the first actor to receive such an honor.

The loss of Sir Irving was a shock, but *Peter Pan* helped propel the West End back into the spotlight. Frohman and Barrie ran the play every Christmas season at the Duke of York's. "The boy who wouldn't grow up" had changed both their lives. For Barrie, the succeeding years were as satisfying as they were stressing. *Peter Pan* had made him internationally famous and considerably richer but personally shattered—his marriage was over. Barrie had found out his wife Mary had been seeing another man whom she would bring to the Barrie summer retreat while Barrie was away. Apparently, Mary misjudged how much the house's staff preferred Barrie over her. They informed the master when Barrie returned. Mary's "guest" never stayed in the guest bedroom, he was told, so Barrie confronted her about it.

It was around this same time that Barrie received a letter from Captain Scott: an invitation to attend baby Peter's christening on October 13, 1909. Scott asked Barrie to be his son's godfather. Barrie was honored and accepted his friend's request, but politely declined being there in person. Instead, he would need to attend his own divorce case.

As Barrie's divorce was being finalized, Scott was signing papers confirming his return to Antarctica. By the time Scott set off, however, in November of 1910, the two friends were not on speaking terms. No one is quite sure why. The most plausible explanation is that Sylvia Llewelyn Davies, the mother of the five boys who played such a vital role in Barrie's life, was dying of cancer, and Scott may have said something about her that troubled Barrie.

The origins of *Peter Pan* are deeply rooted in Barrie's connection to Sylvia, the wife of Arthur Llewelyn Davies and daughter of another novelist, Gerald du Maurier. Barrie and Sylvia met by

James M. Barrie. National Science and Media Museum, U.K. [1898].

chance at a dinner party while she was secretly gathering up sweets in a napkin for youngest son, Peter. Barrie found her delightful and thus began a lifelong friendship. One of the Llewellyn Davies boys, likely Peter, is considered to be the inspiration for Barrie's Peter in the play.

Sylvia would pass away in August of 1910 while Scott was setting off for Antarctica. There were rumors Sylvia and Barrie were linked romantically after the death of Sylvia's husband Arthur Llewelyn Davies three years earlier in 1907, but nothing came of this except Barrie's love for her boys and his desire to protect them. After Sylvia's death, Barrie made good on a promise to become guardian to each of the boys.

Then came Monday, February 10, 1913.

That day was business as usual for Barrie who maintained constant contact either personally or by correspondence with Charles Frohman. The two had been busy planning the yearly production of *Peter Pan* in London, its eighth revival. The bronze statue of Peter Pan had been in Kensington Gardens for about a year and was well received. "Down by the little bay on the southwestern side of the tail of the Serpentine is a May Day gift by J. M. Barrie," the *London Times* declared after its surprise unveiling, "a figure of Peter Pan blowing his pipe on the stump of a tree, with fairies and mice and squirrels all around."

Barrie's mind was on Captain Scott that day. Word had come down that the *Terra Nova* would be docking in New Zealand momentarily and news of the expedition, the first in nearly a year, would be coming shortly. Scott and the rest of the Antarctic crew were expected to be on board.

3

Never ask me to play that again

✐ In January 1913, just as Barrie was anticipating the return of his friend, Kathleen Scott was preparing to sail to New Zealand to see her husband home. Meanwhile, Isadora Duncan arrived in Kiev, Russia, for a six-week engagement to be followed immediately by a tour run in Berlin. The children, Deirdre and Patrick, were staying with her sister Elizabeth, and they all would meet up with Isadora in Germany. Paris Singer was gone, at least for now, having left in a huff after accusing Isadora of seducing another man in her Paris studio bedroom during a party.

In Russia, Isadora was in her element: dancing for appreciative audiences and attending theater productions like *Hamlet* staged by Edward Craig, Deirdre's father. Still, something wasn't right: earlier in the trip, she became ill and fainted, then spent the rest of the day in the hotel room nursing a high fever. A doctor insisted she cancel her performances. "I have the horror of disappointing the public," she told him and went on as scheduled.

During this time, Isadora writes in her memoirs that she experienced visions of dark shadowy figures in her bedroom at night and disturbing hallucinations throughout the day. "Can't you see it?" she asked a friend after seeing coffins on the side of the road. The friend assured her it was just fatigue. Then during an evening's performance she abruptly asked the conductor to play Chopin's

Funeral March. "But why?" he responded curiously. "You have never danced to it."

That night she did. She mimicked a funeral march with slow hesitating steps and arm movements like she was carrying a dead body. "I danced the descent into the grave, and finally the spirit escaping from the imprisoning flesh and rising, rising toward the Light—the Resurrection." When she was finished the crowd sat in stunned silence. Isadora turned to one of the musicians for a reaction. "Never ask me to play that again," he said.

It was the end of January, and she was anxious to leave Russia. "Everything here is freezing," she once wrote about the Moscow winters, "something unthinkable, the cold." Berlin was next. It offered "a new hope," she explained, where at least her children would be waiting for her. Elizabeth arrived as promised with Deirdre and Patrick along with several of Isadora's students who would all dance with her in the capital city. She had been doing the same in Paris. During one performance, the French poet Fernard Divoire noticed something different about the girls. "They are all grown up now," he wrote. "Isadora dances with them and is a part of them. And the delighted audience applauds and applauds, freed of all everyday worries and care, left with no other thoughts but those of grace and youth eternal." He called them quite cleverly, "Les Isadorables."

The Berlin trip and tour was scheduled for financial reasons: Isadora had opened a dancing school and expenses were piling up. Singer and his money were out of the picture for now, so she pleaded for audiences to help her financially. She got mostly a cold response. Berlin was turning on her, thanks to bad publicity and a prudish attitude. Isadora it seemed was now too risqué, and the children who danced with her, exploited. A popular German newspaper proclaimed that the girls were so "scantily clad that their sense of modesty was not protected." Further complicating matters was Isadora's reputation, which had been tarnished recently by incidents reported in the international press. During an American tour, Isadora was accused of "offending the rich" when she told a "privileged" couple in a theater box how she felt about their apparent lack of interest in her performance.

In addition, Isadora's act was no longer unique. More dancers, like the Canadian-born and California-raised Maud Allan, were doing what Isadora was once doing exclusively, but on a much larger stage. Only four years younger than Isadora, Allan had become highly successful dancing in an interpretation of Strauss's opera *Salome,* based on the Oscar Wilde play, and featuring the titillating movement "Dance of the Seven Veils." In 1907, when Strauss premiered the work, it was banned in England, and in America, the Metropolitan Opera House withdrew it from their schedule after several members of the Met's board threatened to quit.

"Exquisitely suggestive, exquisitely evasive, exquisitely graceful," the superlatives came for Allan's performance in *Salome,* curiously from a newspaper in London. "Sawing like a white witch with yearning arms and hands that plead, Miss Allan is such a delicious embodiment of lust that she might win forgiveness with the sins of her wonderful flesh."

Allan never liked comparisons to Isadora although they could not be helped. Unlike Loie Fuller who appreciated the beauty in Isadora's work, as a fellow dancer Allan was more competitive and resentful. Nevertheless, she apparently had no qualms about mimicking Isadora's style in "Vision of Salome," an interpretation piece to the Strauss opera, which played to a packed audience at London's Palace Theatre.

Watching all this unfold was Charles Frohman. As a counter-move to Allan's success at the Palace, he booked Isadora at his own Duke of York's Theatre. Eventually he brought her to America as "The Rage of London," a tour that we already know turned out to be a failure for Frohman and a disappointment for Isadora.

Now in Berlin and later back home in Paris, the strange hallucinations Isadora experienced in Russia still haunted her. She danced the *Funeral March* again; now it was being requested. "After a religious silence," she recalls, "the public remained awed and then applauded wildly. Some women were weeping—some almost hysterical."

Around this time in February of 1913, word was spreading about the crew of the *Terra Nova* returning to New Zealand. Isadora's thoughts must have been with Kathleen and her son Peter. The

Maud Allan. The Library of Congress, part of the Genthe Collection [1916].

two had spent the previous summer together on the French Riviera where Kathleen met her son Patrick and Singer. The sojourn didn't end well. Singer and Isadora fought constantly, and little Patrick got sick. Still, it gave Kathleen time to reflect.

Isadora had a deep respect for Kathleen, though she had a difficult time understanding her friend's devotion to one man. Her own personal relationships with men were equal parts explosive and passionate, but never fully committed. "She chose lovers as she pleased," wrote biographer Peter Kurth, "taking up the gauntlet and staking claim to the timeless privilege of men." One example of this unbridled coquetry, as the French would say, was with George Barnard Shaw, someone she greatly admired and to whom she was introduced by Kathleen. As the story goes, at their first meeting Isadora told Shaw that they should have a baby together on "scientific grounds," clarifying, "one that has my body and your brains."

"Yes, my dear," Shaw retorted, "but suppose it had my body and your brains?"

In her own memoirs, Kathleen recalls that day with an eye roll, to say the least.

The news coming from London was awful. Scott was dead, perishing along with several others in the Antarctic. A telegram from New Zealand confirmed it. "If this is true," wrote a stunned Sir Clements Markham, the famed British exploration financier, "then we have lost the greatest polar explorer that ever lived." Londoners went into mourning. Scott may have been beaten to the pole by Norwegian explorer Roald Amundsen, that everyone knew, but no one was prepared for this. Men went to the extreme reaches of the earth, like the Antarctic, but then came back, as Scott had the first time. Shackleton and, most recently, Amundsen, who had set off a few months before Scott's team, had done the same and returned. In fact, sixty years had passed since someone was lost on the ice. This time it was a different outcome. Scott was arguably as famous as the King of England when he left.

Now he was gone.

4

I have some news for you

⌒◯ On February 14, 1913, only four days after the fate of Captain Scott and the other four unfortunate victims of the *Terra Nova* mission had been announced, a memorial service at St Paul's Cathedral was called to order mostly because the public demanded it. Sir Clements Markham was asked to speak. "We can never hope to see this again," he exclaimed his voice cracking. There were no caskets to carry or gravesite burials to attend. These were souls in spirit only, their bodies never to return. The paper reported at least ten thousand people had lined the streets around the cathedral and estimated there was more gathered that morning than the thousands who had shown up to memorialize the *Titanic* victims just a few months earlier.

The solemnness of the memorial was also tempered by the empathy Londoners felt for the one person who was not there: Scott's wife Kathleen. On that same day in February, while her husband was being memorialized in London, Kathleen Scott was aboard the RMS *Aorangi,* steaming toward New Zealand from its second-to-last stop in Tahiti. While the rest of the world was processing the news of Scott's death, Kathleen was as yet unaware of her husband's fate. Efforts to reach her by telegraph had proven futile. The *Aorangi* had been recently refitted with new first-class berths for passenger comfort, but the radio transmitter was still woefully inept. No messages could be transmitted or received until they ventured closer to the mainland, or at least until another ship could relay a transmission it had already received.

On February 16, two days after the memorial service, a ship headed in the opposite direction of the *Aorangi* passed by in the middle of the night. A message was received. It was news about Scott and the polar crew. The next morning, the ship's radio operator called for the captain. The captain then summoned Kathleen. "I have some news for you but I don't know how to tell you," he said, his hands trembling.

Kathleen asked if it was about the expedition.

He handed her the translated message:

CAPTAIN SCOTT AND SIX OTHERS PERISHED IN BLIZZARD
AFTER REACHING SOUTH POLE JANUARY 18.

"Oh well...I expected that," she said. "Thanks very much. I will go and think about it." Kathleen later said she did not want to make a scene or upset any of her fellow travelers. She left the captain and went down to a scheduled Spanish lesson then prepared for lunch. She didn't tell anyone the news. "For an hour and a half, I acquitted myself quite well," she wrote. Later, she returned to the captain's quarters and asked him not to alarm the other passengers with the news. Only the officers knew, he assured her.

Kathleen spent the next several days occupying her mind by reading and playing deck golf. "Anything to get the awful picture out of my head," she wrote. The ship was still too far to receive transmissions, so Kathleen had no idea how Scott and the others had died. Even the initial message was wrong; only five had perished not six. "All these long, weary nights without news," she wrote in her diary.

The man who had reached the pole first, Roald Amundsen, received a similar cable in Norway. "Died in a blizzard?" Amundson was generally surprised. "Although we had thought our party well prepared for eventualities, we had understood that Captain Scott's preparations were the most perfect and modern of any polar exploration," he stated. Amundsen was right. Scott and his team were well-equipped for the journey, but time and weather conspired to work against them.

On February 20th, the *Aorangi* reached its final stop of Raro-tonga in the South Pacific. The island had a post office where a cable had been received for Mrs. Scott from the crew of the *Terra Nova*. It contained sympathies but no additional information. Kathleen spent the days ashore reading and writing in her diary while sitting on the coral rocks and watching the surf come in at sunset. "The nights are beautiful with the moon," she wrote, "and all the different aspects of [Scott's death] come to me one by one. The agony of leaving his job undone, losing the other lives, and leaving us uncared for, must have been unspeakable." On Febru-ary 23, the *Aorangi* was close enough to New Zealand to receive messages. Kathleen sat in the wireless room anticipating each one. "Messages of condolence," she wrote, "lovely messages, keep com-ing through, coming and coming without ceasing."

Finally on Thursday, February 27, the *Aorangi* docked in Wel-lington, New Zealand's capital, on the southern tip of the North Island and nearly five hundred miles north from Lyttelton where the *Terra Nova* had returned earlier in the month to pick up sup-plies. Dr. Edward Atkinson was there to greet her. Atkinson was Scott's handpicked doctor on the mission and someone who could conduct important scientific experiments on parasites, a passion Atkinson picked up while studying medicine in the Royal Navy. There was a biologist, a geologist, and a zoologist on the crew, but Atkinson was the only parasitologist. Atkinson was also part of the original team that set out on the ice, but halfway across, Scott changed plans. Fearing more risk, Scott decided that only four others and he would march to the pole. Atkinson and several other men would go back to camp and become a search-and-rescue party if Scott failed to return. Now the ship was back in New Zealand, and it was Atkinson's duty to relay the sad details to Scott's wife.

Atkinson told Kathleen that on April 1, 1912, it became apparent that Scott's team was not going to make it back before the win-ter season set in. After the daylight returned in early September, plans were made to organize a rescue team, but traveling long dis-tances would be limited by the changing season. Atkinson decided that in order to safely reach Scott's party or learn more of their whereabouts, the team needed to check the depot locations where

Edgar "Taff" Evans. The Library of Congress, part of the prints and photographs divison. Herbert Pointing, photographer claimant [1910-1911].

supplies were cached. Blizzards continued to kick up and temperatures rose to zero. After stalling out at several depot points, they trudged back to Cape Evans. It was the first of May and darkness had set in.

By August the sun had returned. Headed by the mules and dogs, the journey south to find Scott and his crew began on October 29. Atkinson took along two other men, Ashley Cherry-Garrard and Silas Wright. "The surface was extremely good—hard, and almost marbled—and the sledges followed the animals easily," he explained. They were making twelve miles a day. On November 10, they reached One Ton Depot, the largest of all the supply chains, and stopped for a half day's rest.

On November 12, as they marched twelve miles south of One Ton Depot, the party spotted the top of a tent sticking out of the snow. The tent was completely snowed over and outside were Scott's skis and several long bamboo sticks used to mast the sledges. They managed to push enough snow aside to reach the entrance of the outside shell. Finally, after more digging, Atkinson was able to pull aside the tent's inner flap. Inside were three men wrapped in their sleeping bags. One had his arms crossed over his chest; another was peacefully tucked in. It was Edward Wilson and Henry Bowers. In the middle was Captain Scott. His body lay half out of the bag with one arm stretched out over Wilson.

Near the bodies was a journal in Scott's handwriting. It told the story of how Edgar Evans, known to the crew as "Taff," died at the foot of the Beardmore Glacier. The fifth member of the pole party, Lieutenant Lawrence Oates had walked out of the tent willingly. About eighteen miles south of the tent, Atkinson's team would find Oates's sleeping bag, but not his body, which they assumed had been covered over with snow. Before departing, Atkinson pulled out the burial service lesson from his pocket and held a short service, reading from Corinthians and singing "Onward Christian Soldiers." Then the three men collapsed the tent over the bodies as they lay, piled up snow in a mound, and, using Scott's own ski poles, made a makeshift cross on top.

5

Be your happy self again

⤵ Kathleen spent the next several days accepting sympathies from the surviving crew members who had stayed behind in New Zealand until she arrived. Mrs. Scott wasn't the only widow there. "Mrs. Wilson is behaving very well, poor, poor soul," she recalled. "She was sweet and genteel. I am so glad we could be nice to each other. It is comforting for the both of us, I think."

If Kathleen saw Hilda Evans, wife of Scott's second-in-command Edward "Teddy" Evans, in Wellington she does not mention it. Hilda's circumstances were much different than Kathleen's. She had her husband back. In fact, the previous year Hilda had spent several months nursing Evans back to health after he returned to New Zealand with the *Terra Nova* in January of 1912, diagnosed with scurvy. Like Dr. Atkinson, Evans thought he would accompany Scott on the final team, but when Scott turned several parties back, Evans was trusted to lead the split crew back to safety.

During the trip back to camp, Evans became gravely ill. He had to be strapped to a sled and dragged the rest of the way. Since Evans could not fulfill his duties as second-in-command, by order of rank Dr. Atkinson was put in charge of the crew awaiting Scott's return. Atkinson made his first order an important one: sending a frail, but still alive, Evans back with the *Terra Nova*, which was set to return to New Zealand for supplies. Hilda nursed Teddy back

Terra Nova. The Library of Congress, part of the prints and photographs division. Herbert Pointing, photographer [1910 or 1911].

to health. Nearly a year later, when the *Terra Nova* was ready to launch again, Evans was ready to guide it. Although it was under difficult circumstances, he guided the ship back to Antarctica and safely picked up the surviving crew members.

Kathleen felt no kinship with Hilda Evans and didn't know Teddy personally, but that was beside the point now. Even if Kathleen had sought them out in New Zealand, the reunited couple, she was told, left rather quickly.

In addition to Scott's journal, Kathleen sorted through letters he wrote to loved ones in his final days. They were all personal and touching. His letters to Kathleen were written in an apologetic tone. "I wasn't a very good husband," he wrote. "But I hope I shall be a good memory." He mentions Peter: "Certainly the end is nothing for you to be ashamed of and I like to think that the boy will have a good start, his parentage of which he may be proud. You see I'm anxious for you and the boy's future. Make the boy interested in natural history if you can. It is better than games. Try and make him believe in God, it is comforting."

He tells Kathleen to remarry and "be your happy self again."

According to Scott's journal, the final days were a race against the forces of nature. After reaching the South Pole, the crew of five prepared for the grueling eight-hundred-mile journey back to the safety of camp. "All the daydreams must go," Scott summarized. "It will be a wearisome return. Now for the run home and a desperate struggle, I wonder if we can do it." Scott knew they were chasing the weather and the unavoidable delays cost them precious time. Every time they made some progress they were stopped by the cold and wind. Their physical conditions were rapidly deteriorating, especially their feet. These were so severely ravaged by frostbite that it made walking nearly impossible. Eventually, it was just too much to overcome.

Among all the letters Scott wrote, there was one Kathleen did not open. It was given to her to forward. She immediately had it sent.

Scott had addressed it to James M. Barrie.

Kathleen returned to London and to Peter and continued with her work, including plans for a larger-than-life statue of her husband shown standing defiantly in his artic gear with a ski pole in one hand. Then in April, she received some news about Hilda and Teddy Evans. Teddy Evans was heading back to London by train. When she found out why, she rushed to meet him.

A month before, Evans and Hilda had left New Zealand on the *Aorangi* and sailed to Sydney where they spent a quiet week together. From there, they boarded the ship *Ortanio* for a leisurely cruise along Italy's coastline. On the cruise, Hilda complained of stomach pain. Evans thought she might have a severe case of seasickness. As the *Ortanio* continued, Hilda got worse. Evans called for the ship's doctor who in turn called for a surgeon from Melbourne who was traveling with them. The surgeon diagnosed Hilda with peritonitis and performed an emergency procedure. By the time the *Ortanio* reached the Naples port, there was hope: Hilda was conscious and alert. But when the ship set back out to sea, her condition deteriorated. She died at midnight on April 18 with Evans by her side. Evans often said that he went to Antarctica to make his wife proud. "With a heavy heart," he wrote after her death, "I have no one to work for." Hilda was buried in the next port stop of Toulon. The ship's officers served as pallbearers.

When Evans's train pulled into the London station, Kathleen was there. "Lady Scott with true womanly sympathy, made a special journey to Charing Cross and waited for more than an hour in order to greet Commander Evans and to offer him in his time of sorrow a word of comfort and a welcome," the *London Times* reported. "The meeting between the widow and the widower was a touching scene."

Hilda's unfortunate death, however, wasn't as personal as the news Kathleen had received just a week before from Paris.

It was about her friend Isadora Duncan.

6

They never had
a sorrow

⟡ "It can't be true," Isadora told Paris Singer who was on buckled knees, crying uncontrollably at her feet. Just minutes before Singer had surprised Isadora by appearing in the doorway of an empty rehearsal space where she was awaiting the arrival of students. "Try to calm down," she said. But there was no consoling him. Singer knew what Isadora refused to believe.

"The children are dead," he told her.

Isadora recalled the events of just a short time earlier. She had put Deirdre and Patrick in the Renault automobile after the governess Annie Sim insisted they return home to rest. It was a glorious afternoon. Singer had recently returned to her life and was in a jolly mood. He asked to meet them all and they had a nice lunch together, but Isadora had a scheduled rehearsal planned in the evening. "Will you come in with the children and wait?" she asked the governess, hoping they would all ride back together. The governess, however, insisted the children should go. Isadora reluctantly agreed. "I will return soon," she promised. Then she went inside to wait for her students.

It was just a few hundred yards down the road where the horrible scene played out. The Renault made a sudden stop to avoid a collision and stalled at an intersection along the banks of the Seine River. The driver, Isadora's personal chauffer, got out to crank the car. When the engine turned over the vehicle leaped forward, continued down a grassy slope, and jumped the embankment into the Seine. The chauffer ran to stop it. He reached for the running board with outstretched hands but fell to the ground instead. Within minutes the car was submerged. Several patrons at a terrace café nearby jumped in the water. They kept going under and kept coming back up empty. Police and firemen arrived and continued the desperate search. A motorboat was brought in and with ropes and anchors pulled the car out. "There was a heart-rending scene when the door of the car was opened and the bodies of the children were found clinging to their dead nurse," the *London Times* reported. "The witnesses and even the firemen, well-accustomed to scenes of tragedy, couldn't restrain their tears."

It was April 19, 1913.

Isadora stayed inside for the next three full days. She neither slept nor changed clothes. Her students came and decorated her gardens "with all the white flowers they could find in Paris," a friend wrote. Singer was reportedly so crestfallen he checked himself into a clinic. Friends and acquaintances came to her studio some even making it through the doors to personally offer their sympathies to Isadora as she lay stoically on the couch. Others just stood outside and reflected. The children's playthings were still strewn about the yard.

Although they weren't very close personally, Mrs. Pat Campbell always felt a certain kinship with Isadora after she had discovered her by chance, destitute and dancing, near her Kensington Square home. She helped jump-start a career that arguably grew to be more successful than her own. While there is no record of Mrs. Pat sending a condolence to Isadora directly, she did mention the tragedy in one of her published letters to George Bernard Shaw: "I open the paper to read of Isadora Duncan's heart-ending sorrow...poor Singer...poor Ellen Terry, poor [Edward] Gordon Craig...poor all of us that have hearts to ache."

The funeral was on April 22 at Isadora's home studio. Just about everyone in Paris who was famous was there. During a brief ceremony Isadora felt the weight of the moment. As she approached the open caskets her knees weakened and she collapsed. Witnesses

Isadora Duncan with Deidre and Patrick. New York Public Library, from
the Jerome Robbins Dance Division [1912].

say she got up, regained her composure, thanked those who attended, and ascended the spiral staircase to the third-floor gallery where her close friend Mary Desti said she collapsed again. Singer also broke down at the funeral, telling everyone how much he loved both the children as his own. Conspicuous in his absence was Deidre's father, Edward Craig. After receiving a cable from Isadora, he sent a heartfelt letter to her but asked a friend to go to the funeral in his place. "I don't know yet how to think or feel," he wrote.

A large procession traveled from the studio across the city to a crematorium at Père Lachaise on the hallowed grounds where Frederic Chopin and Oscar Wilde were interred. "No tears," Isadora told Desti on the ride to the cemetery. "They never had a sorrow, and we must not have a sorrowful today."

Days later, Isadora would leave Paris and go to the Greek Islands to clear her mind. There she would meet her brother Raymond who had set up a charitable relief effort for thousands of homeless refuges. "The whole country is in need," he told her. "Come and help to feed the children...comfort the women." Before she left, Singer paid her a visit at the studio. Although Isadora requested no visitors, Desti let him in. She knew he was the only one who could comfort her.

After the shock of the tragedy subsided and Isadora left Paris, there was still one unanswered question being murmured by the press and whispered among her many admirers.

Perhaps it was just too soon to ask.

Would she ever dance again?

7

Let's do a play together

꩜ Now in his fifties and enjoying the rewards of a successful career, theater manager Charles Frohman could afford a little more time to relax and unwind. The appointments in New York City were far too frenzied for any peaceful interludes, so Frohman chose the English countryside instead. In London, the Savoy Hotel was normally where he stayed, entertained, and made important deals, but his favorite place to spend some quiet downtime was a cozy cottage in Marlow, a sleepy little village on the River Thames, about thirty miles west of Central London.

Those who knew him best knew it was a weekend ritual for Frohman. Every Saturday he would take a train to Slough, then continue by automobile to Marlow. His driver would be Pauline Chase, whom Frohman handpicked in 1906 as the third actress to play Peter Pan. After giving her the role, they developed a close relationship. Frohman took Chase under his wing and mentored her. He became like a father figure to her, and for Frohman, who never married nor had any children of his own, she was like the daughter he never had. Frohman had purchased a scenic cottage in the Tree Tops section of Marlow where Chase would stay, and every Saturday, like clockwork, when Frohman was in London, he would join her there.

On weekends in Marlow, Frohman would linger in the garden,

take walks, and catch up on his reading. During the day, Frohman and Chase would visit antique shops on Marlow's one long street. For Frohman it was as far away from Broadway as he could get. For the Marlow locals, it was business as usual. To them Frohman wasn't that larger-than-life American theater manager but just someone who kindly "inquired about their babies and who had a big generous nature."

This pleased Frohman who tried to avoid being the center of attention. According to his oldest brother Daniel, young Charles was fearfully shy as a boy. Even as an adult, Frohman was still uncomfortable in front of a large audience and refused all invitations to events in which he was the one being honored. "Charles cared nothing about honors." And, his brother added, "He was content to hide behind the mask of his activities." That's why Marlow and the little cottage were so special to him. Oftentimes, he would just sit for hours on the porch, listening to the birds and smoking. In the evening he would retire to his room and pick over a manuscript before going to bed.

In 1914, Frohman became ill and was laid up for weeks in his New York residence at the Knickerbocker Hotel. He was fifty-eight and at the peak of his career with nearly three dozen "stars" under his management. Still, one aspect of his personal and professional life gnawed at him. David Belasco, whose play *The Stranglers of Paris* the two had staged together years ago at the Madison Square Theatre, was out of his life. They had been estranged for twelve years. Frohman never liked to hold grudges. Even actresses like Mrs. Pat, with whom he disagreed, and Isadora Duncan, who he failed to make his American star, maintained constant contact. You never left Charles Frohman.

This breach with Belsaco, for whatever reason, was unsettling. Fortunately for Frohman, Belasco was thinking the same thing. As the story goes, when Belasco heard Frohman was sick in bed, he said, "C.F. is lying ill at the Knickerbocker? I must go see him." He started to write a note of well wishes when the phone rang. It was Frohman. "He wants to see you," an associate told Belasco. When Belasco went to see him, Frohman raised a hand to his old friend.

"Let's do a play together," he told him. Belsaco agreed at once.

Frohman recovered and the two men stuck to their word. The play was a revival of Belasco's *A Celebrated Case,* and it opened in Boston before returning to the Empire Theatre in New York. The newly reunited team was big news. When the opening night's final curtain call included the request for the playwright and producer to join the actors in taking a bow, Belasco took his turn, but no persuasion on anyone's part could convince Frohman to step on stage.

Frohman ended 1914 with a curious choice, a play titled *The Hyphen* by Justus Miles Forman regarding the loyalty of German-Americans. The German debate was already stirring in real life thanks to the war that was brewing overseas. America was not involved, at least not yet, but attitudes toward German immigrants and descendants of immigrants living in the United States were contentious at best. Frohman, being an American born to German immigrants, received threatening letters during rehearsals. He vehemently disagreed with the protests and felt the play showed a side of ignorance that spurred patriotism, not lessened it. Frohman took a special interest in making sure it was successful. He felt he was doing a national service by producing it. "AMERICA FIRST," Frohman put in large letters at the top of the play's stage bill.

When the play was finally revealed in April of 1915, a group of mostly pro-Germany supporters packed the theater and disrupted the performance numerous times. Outside explosions could be heard—possibly pipe bombs going off, people feared. Thankfully, it was only construction on the subway nearby. The night ended peacefully, but the play was forever tarnished. Frohman's confidence in it waned too. After a brief run, he shut it down.

However, Frohman and *The Hyphen's* playwright, Justus Forman, remained close. "I want you to come to England with me and meet James Barrie and some of my English friends," Frohman told him. Frohman had planned to sail to England sometime that summer, but plans had changed. Barrie had contacted him in late April and asked that he leave early so he could help with a play Barrie had written.

Justus Miles Forman. The Library of Congress, part of the Bain Collection [1910–1915].

8

I shan't forget the
Peter of the Past

⌒ℐꝋ When Charles Frohman last saw Barrie in April of 1914 something had changed in the man who created *Peter Pan.* For one, he had become infatuated with a French chorus girl named Gaby Deslys. Why Barrie was so attracted to Deslys is a bit puzzling. In the theater world, she stood for everything for which Barrie did not. Nevertheless, he found her captivating. Barrie invited Deslys over for tea at his home and told her she was going to be his next big star. It was a page right out of Frohman's playbook and Barrie was determined to make it work. The problem was, while Deslys was a media darling, appearing in all the right places, dressing in fine clothing, and always sporting a large billowy hat—the fashion statement of the day—she was not an established actress. Barrie had this to offer her at least. He had been dabbling in writing music revues himself, lighthearted affairs mostly, including a strange ditty he titled *Hullo Ragtime!*

In 1914, Barrie told Frohman all his big ideas, including an innovative new project for Deslys that would feature something completely different in his repertoire: cinematography. His scheme was this: Deslys would appear in a half dozen sketches and projected behind her would be a large screen where short film sequences of audience reactions would show. The candid shots would come from cameras placed in the hall and edited into the sequences on stage.

"Can you imagine for example," Barrie told Frohman, "the thirty-foot face of England's Prime Minster Asquith behind Deslys as she does one of her suggestive dances?" He called it "Cinema Supper" and proposed they stage it at the Savoy Hotel.

In the months following the announcement of Scott's death, Barrie occupied his time by focusing on a project called *The Adored One*. He had an actress in mind to play the lead role, someone he knew through his friend George Bernard Shaw: Mrs. Pat Campbell.

Mrs. Pat had great faith in Barrie, and they got along well. She found the play funny and charming. Meanwhile, Frohman was ecstatic. He had Barrie back at his Duke of York's Theatre where the magic started for them both. It was a surefire hit, Frohman thought.

Only it was not.

Barrie had recently experienced a series of flops and *The Adored One* was another. This time it was worse: not only had he failed in London, he had failed at the theater that made *Peter Pan* famous.

During scenes where Barrie thought the audience would laugh, they gasped instead. Moreover, no one was buying the premise that a mother, Leonora, Mrs. Pat's role, could push a man out of a railroad carriage door to his death and get away with it. Mrs. Pat, however, in her memoirs found the part of Leonora "lovely." She identified with a mother's intuition when it came to protecting her children. In this case, Leonora politely asks the man to close the window because her daughter has a cold. When he refuses, she lashes out. As absurd as that it is, the audience just didn't get that the play was intended to be a spoof.

When it was over, boos not cheers came from the confused crowd. "That Sir James Barrie–J. M. Barrie, the author of *Peter Pan* and *The Little Minister*–should be booed in a London theater where he has so often triumphed is an incident whose echoes have reverberated throughout Great Britain like a thunderclap from a Blue Sky," the *New York Times* reported.

Barrie never blamed his actors for the opening night debacle, only himself. He went backstage to tell Mrs. Pat such. "No one has worked as well for me before," he told her. Then he set about to fix this thing he created. He changed a courtroom scene into a dream sequence, added a love scene, and, with some nifty darkening effects, gave the audience the feeling that no murder had taken place after all. Leonora didn't kill anyone.

Barrie let the revised version continue for ten weeks before shutting it down.

The failure of *The Adored One* was a setback for Barrie, and Scott's death was still weighing heavily on his mind. His health was also a concern, and others noticed that he started using a walking stick in public.

While he worked to right a string of failures, Barrie kept up his correspondence with Kathleen Scott. Only weeks after the awful news arrived from Antarctica, Barrie received a letter sent by Kathleen that was written by Captain Scott in his final days. The poignant letter contained a passage about watching over Kathleen and Peter. "I want you to help my widow and my boy, your godson," Scott wrote. Barrie took it to heart. In January of 1914, he sent Peter a playfully written letter: "My Dear Peter, Hallo...It is time u sawed *Peter Pan.* I am to ring your mother up about it tomorrow. He is brave he can fly. I am yure loving Godfather."

As promised, the next day, Barrie took little Peter Scott to see *Peter Pan,* now in its tenth revival at the Duke of York's Theatre. Barrie's niece, Madge Murray, had now replaced Pauline Chase in the lead role. That year, Chase had gotten married to a dashing cricketer and banker named Alex Drummond whom Barrie claimed Frohman and he had introduced to her. Barrie's emotions were evident in a letter he sent that day to Chase. "I'm going to the P. Pan performance today, and I hope all is well, but you needn't be afraid. I shan't forget the Peter of the Past."

Also preying on his mind that day was George Llewelyn Davies, the oldest of the five Llewelyn Davies boys. He was heading off to fight in France only months after England declared war on Germany. Barrie was especially close to George and his departure was an emotional one. Before deploying out in December, Barrie gave him a "kit" of goodies, including the book *The Little White Bird,* which introduced the world to Peter Pan. Three months later on March 15, 1915, while trying to drive the Germans out of the French town of St. Eloi, Second Lieutenant George Llewe-lyn Davies was shot in the head and killed instantly. Barrie got the news in the middle of the night. He woke up the children's long-time nanny Mary Hodgsen who was still watching over the young-est Llewelyn Davies boy, Nicholas, who was eleven.

"This dreadful war will get them all in the end," Barrie told her.

Barrie had been writing to George on the front and telling him all about his plans for Gaby Deslys, with whom Barrie suspected George had been romantically involved before leaving. "I expect the burlesque should be on in about three weeks," he wrote. Bar-rie had written a revue for Deslys titled *Rosy Rapture, or the Pride of the Beauty Chorus* and rehearsals were set to start soon.

On March 22, seven days after George's death, *Rosy Rapture* opened at the Duke of York's. It was billed as two Barrie plays in one. *The New World* was a short one-act play Barrie had written to precede the main event. Neither one had much impact. Despite Deslys's elaborate costumes and another film projection gimmick that Barrie incorporated into the dancing scenes, the play received negative reviews and generated poor audience response. Barrie didn't want another failure on his hands. By April, he felt only one man might be able to fix it. He wired Charles Frohman in New York and asked him to come at once.

Frohman cabled back that he was on his way.

German submarines in the harbor. The Library of Congress, part of the Bain Collection [1914-1915].

Act IV

⌒✍⌒ "History is a lively abode, full of surprises." *—Erik Larson*

In January of 1918, only eight months after the United States entered World War I, a new movie opened titled *Lest We Forget* and starred Rita Jolivet, a popular actress at the time. Jolivet played Rita Heriot, a French opera singer and telegraph operator who gets tangled up in an espionage plot.

In the silent film, punctuated by text frames, the fictional Heriot is captured by the Germans and sentenced to die. She manages to escape prison and plans a reunion in America with the man who loves her, a New York billionaire named Harry Winslow. Unbeknownst to Heriot, however, Winslow has left New York and enlisted in the French Army to avenge her suspected death.

Meanwhile, a German diplomat who has fallen madly in love with Heriot has some bad news: Winslow is dead, killed in the Battle of Marne.

He begs Heriot to stay with him.

But Winslow is not dead, only injured.

Heriot goes to America as planned to revive her singing career.

At this point in the movie the viewer is duped into believing Heriot is safe. But the diplomat is still in contact, and Heriot tells him that she plans to sail to London for more stage work.

He tells her to stay in America.

The diplomat knows something that Heriot does not: the ship to England is targeted by German forces for attack. Because he cannot reveal the truth that might save her life, Heriot boards the ship to certain doom. Or so it seems.

The tension plays out dramatically and tragically. The audience, while captivated by the realism of the disaster scenes, is relieved when Heriot and Winslow are reunited in a happy ending.

But there was more to *Lest We Forget* than just the story. There was a personal side to the movie just as compelling—and everyone knew it.

Just a few years earlier, Rita Jolivet, the actress, had actually been on board an ocean liner headed for London when it was torpedoed by the Germans. Thus in playing the screen role of the French girl in peril, Jolivet was in a very real sense reliving and re-creating her own brush with death.

1
Ah, Carmen.
My adored Carmen

᭣᭣ One night backstage at the Opéra Comique Theatre in Paris, Mary Garden, a French sopranist, was freshening up during intermission of another performance of the opera, *Aphrodite*. The part of Chrysis was a challenging but rewarding one for Garden and the sold-out crowd was enjoying every seductive minute. Garden had other reasons to be pleased. For three weeks, while visiting London, she lay in bed at the Savoy Hotel wrecked by a bout of laryngitis and tonsillitis, wondering if she would ever perform again. Now healthy and ready to be back on stage, she returned to France where *Aphrodite* awaited her.

Born in Aberdeen, Scotland, in February of 1874, Garden was one of four siblings, all girls. She was the second to arrive. Her father, Robert Davidson Garden, described as an athlete and an engineer, left Scotland for a year alone in New York, then came back for the family after establishing a business there. Little Mary was only five at the time, and she could sing.

The family settled in Brooklyn before moving to Chicopee, Massachusetts. From there they went to Chicago where Garden stayed until she left for Paris at the age of sixteen. Garden had seen an opera at the Auditorium Theatre in Chicago, an interpretation of Shakespeare's *Romeo and Juliet* by French composter Charles

Gounod and heard the famous Australian sopranist Nellie Melba for the first time. She wanted to be like Nellie.

"I sailed away to a new life," Garden recalls about the trip to France. "I never saw America again until I came back as an established artist."

Although she didn't know it at the time, her journey back to America would begin in 1906 in that dressing room of the Opéra Comique Theatre while preparing for the third act of *Aphrodite*. She heard a knock on the door. Garden demanded the unseen visitor to leave. "No one is allowed at intermission," she insisted. A card was slipped through the door. It had a name on it...an American theater manager she did not recognize: Oscar Hammerstein.

"Have him call me tomorrow at my home," she instructed from behind the closed door. But the next day no call came. Garden forgot all about the card until the following year when she was walking home from the Opéra Comique on a beautiful spring day and found someone waiting for her inside her drawing room. It was Oscar Hammerstein. "Turn around, Mary," he said, "and let me see your figure."

Garden laughed. "Unlike all the other impresarios I have ever known with their usual questions about what operas I've sung and how much money do I want," she later reflected on their initial meeting, "Oscar only wanted to know what I looked like from behind."

She granted his request with flair.

The two worked out a contract. Garden would go to America and become the lead sopranist at the Manhattan Opera House. Hammerstein had opened it less than a year earlier to compete with the more established Metropolitan Opera House. "I left for America with thirty trunks and a dog," she explained.

Once ashore, she had some work to do. She was new and French dramas needed some introduction. Hammerstein was patient. So was Garden. "It's ridiculous to let any criticism down you," she thought. "I don't care what it is, it is the public that matters." Eventually the New York press warmed up to Garden. One writer for the *New York Times*, James Huneker wrote a full-page article about her.

Mary Garden. The Library of Congress, part of the Bain Collection [1913].

"MARY GARDEN, SUPERWOMAN" was the headline.

In New York, among her many successes, Garden would revive the great French opera *Carmen,* perhaps the most-beloved opera of all time. The packed houses night after night confirmed it. The story of a gypsy girl pursued by two men, a soldier and a bullfighter, who in the end loses her own life from their jealous love, proved as popular in America as it had in France.

For Garden, the operas were also personal. She had close working relationships with many of the men who wrote the music she was performing, including the French composer, Claude Debussy, who gave her *Pelléas et Mélisande,* his only opera. The man who gave *Carmen* its music, however, was not one of them.

That's because Georges Bizet was dead.

Let's go back, long before Mary Garden's revival in America, in October of 1874, when *Carmen* opened in Paris to a less-than-enthusiastic response. Much of the criticism wasn't aimed at Bizet's music but upon the story itself, a novella written by Prosper Mérimée. The central character of Carmen was simply considered too disreputable for the sympathy she was expected to receive. The production itself, especially the scene in which Carmen gets stabbed by the jealous soldier, was also debated. "Please try not to have her die," one of the two directors of the Opéra Comique Theatre, Adolph de Leuven pleaded. "Death on the stage of the Opéra Comique! Such a thing has never been seen—never."

Ludovic Halévy, the other director, offered a truce. The death scene would be bathed in a bright sunlight and amidst the celebration of the bullfights. The ensuing murder, while shocking, would be shrouded by crowds and chaos. "Ah, Carmen. My adored Carmen," the soldier cries. "You can arrest me. I was the one who killed her." This was still not enough for de Leuven. "Don't make her die," was his final demand. Then he quit.

Bizet worked through the director's squabbles. He completed the score and secured the singers. He picked the French-born mezzo-sopranist Célestine Galli-Marié to play Carmen. Based on the play's success, Galli-Marié is still famous even today for being the first to play that role. She was thirty-eight at the time and a mainstay at the Opéra Comique since 1866. Her initial reaction to being offered the part of *Carmen* seems to echo the sentiments of those who were unfamiliar with Mérimée's story.

"What is it?" she asked.

Finally in September, *Carmen* was ready for rehearsals. When it opened in October it was already being talked about. Trying to avoid scandal, the producer Camille Du Locle kept the usual family audience out. He invited those who were intellectually tuned to musical theater, especially operas: fellow composers, producers, friends of the cast and crew, and admirers of Bizet. The plan worked up to a point. While the first half was well received, by the fourth and final act the response was, as one writer called it, "a glacier." Based on the lack of affirmation backstage, Bizet thought it was a flop. He humbly apologized. He felt the audience did not understand the work, and, as good composers often do, he set out to improve it. Eight months later, and after only thirty-two performances, Bizet took a cold-water swim in the Seine River, suffered a heart attack and fever, and died on June 3, 1875, at the age of thirty-six.

Things started to change for *Carmen,* particularly after Bizet's death. "What had my friends been talking about?" an acquaintance of Bizet's, Pierre Berton, explained after missing opening night and seeing another performance. "Here tonight, I was not alone under a spell." That's why today, *Carmen* is one of the world's most popular and identifiable operas. Even those who know little about the history of operatic theater recognize its name. Many know just the music alone, a success attributed to Georges Bizet—posthumously, of course, because he never lived to see it.

His son, however, did.

Jacques Bizet was only three when his father passed, but the reverberations of *Carmen's* success, especially for the son of the man who was lauded for it, would last a lifetime—and not in a good way. Suffering the sting of rejection for not being like his father musically, he eventually succumbed to the pressure by ending his own life at the age of fifty.

In between, however, was a fascinating life.

After his father's death, the young Bizet continued in school but was now known as the son of the late-great composer of *Carmen*. Although he was described as a troublemaker in the classroom, he was not punished. "With a famous name like yours," the schoolmaster informed him, "you will never be expelled."

Although there was pressure to follow in his father's footsteps and create works like *Carmen*, Bizet could not write music, though he could write stories that could be set to music. This pleased some, but for others it wasn't enough. Still, he honored his father's memory and sought to solidify his heritage. As an adult, Bizet went to see *Carmen* as often as he could and marveled at one singer in particular, Mary Garden.

In her memoir written in 1951, Garden mentions performing *Carmen* in New York but not in Paris. If Bizet claims to have gone to many of her performances, *Carmen* or not, the two most likely met at some point. He was after all the famous son of Georges Bizet and looked uncannily like his father. "There standing in front of me, in all his sturdy independence, was, I imagined, Georges Bizet himself," a friend once wrote about Jacques's appearance.

Having never met the man who made the role of Carmen so important to her, Garden would likely have been ambivalent. Five years younger than Jacques Bizet, she wasn't even born yet when Georges died. She did, however, have a story to tell that came from a friend, Benjamin Godard. After the first night performance of *Carmen*, Godard, also a composer, went backstage to offer Bizet his well wishes. He was one of the few who congratulated him that night on the success of *Carmen*. Bizet was confused. "Success!?," he questioned. "Don't you see that these bourgeois have not understood a word of my work I have written for them?" Godard then told Garden that Bizet left and wandered the streets of Paris until dawn. "A day or two later," Godard relayed, "he had sufficiently regained his equilibrium to take steps to improve the performance of *Carmen*."

Jacques Bizet attended two years of medical school at the University of Paris that went nowhere. He eventually started a literary magazine with another writer friend Marcel Proust and a cousin his own age Daniel Halévy, the son of Ludovic Halévy, the Opéra Comique director who fought to keep *Carmen's* death scene un-

Georges Bizet. The Library of Congress, part of the Bain Collection [1860-1875].

touched. The magazine titled *Le Banquet* didn't attract enough readers and faded away within a year. Bizet, however, continued to write. He crafted a few noticeable plays and burlesque-type shows and was lauded for his wit, but that was all. He did not write any dramas. Eventually, his father's legacy, along with a deep depression and two marriages—one that ended sadly with the death of his first wife Madeleine at an early age, and another that ended in divorce—sent him spiraling into a darkness from which he never recovered. On November 3, 1922, he put a gun in his mouth and pulled the trigger.

The French press was mournful but mostly apathetic. More emphasis was on Bizet's mother Geneviève, with whom he shared a complicated relationship after his father's death. She had lost both her husband and son. The fact of his suicide was concealed from the public. A week later, Bizet's writer friend Marcel Proust passed away unexpectedly from illness.

Four years later, in 1926, Geneviève died at the age of seventy-seven.

Mary Garden eventually became a U.S. citizen and lived long enough to witness the start of the Vietnam War, President Kennedy's assassination, and the Beatles first trip to America. She died in January of 1967 at the age of ninety-two. But these endings are not as important as something else that was just beginning to emerge while Jacques Bizet and the others were still alive—the rise of the motorcar.

As it turns out, beyond music, the name Bizet has an interesting tie to its history.

2

Always an Amilcar

∽ In 1894 at the Salon du Cycle exhibition in Paris, all of two motor vehicles were on display for the public to view. As it was, there were only twenty cars total in all of France. There was little interest. The next year, Paris hosted a car race and although skeptical about the future of "self-driven carriages" as they were known to some, French president Felix Faure attended, arriving and leaving as he always did in a horse-drawn buggy.

The 1,178-kilometer- (732-mile-) Paris-Bordeaux-Paris Trail is considered the very first motor race of its kind, though it ended rather conspicuously: the vehicle that crossed the finish line first was denied the top prize. Although driver Émile Levassor in his Panhard et Levassor completed the course in just shy of forty-nine hours at an average speed of just short of twenty-five miles per hour, the rules of the race strictly stated that only four-seated vehicles would be honored, and the Panhard et Levassor was a two-seater. Whether Levassor knew this or not when he started is unclear. Either way, he was disqualified.

Six hours later another two-seated vehicle crossed the finish line –impressive, but again ineligible. Finally, five hours later driver Paul Koechlin finished the race in a Peugeot, a four-seater. Technically, he finished third, but he was the first qualifying car to complete the race. By then, it was rather anticlimactic. The next year

Martha Ferrare sur Amilcar. The Bibliothèque nationale de France, part of the Gallica Digital Library, public domain [1924].

the rules were changed: the fastest car, no matter how many seats it had, would be declared the winner.

The man responsible for organizing the spectacle was the renowned French automobilist Marquis Jules-Albert de Dion. Based on the interest generated by the races, he decided to put on a show to display vehicles to the public. To qualify, a short race by comparison, only 40 kilometers from Versailles to Paris, had to be completed for participation.

In 1898, the first Paris Motor Show opened. With 269 exhibits it showcased the biggest French motor vehicle makers at the time: Peugeot, Panhard et Levassor, and Daimler-Benz. Mostly curiosity seekers came to see the vehicles that first year. Next year attendance doubled. To this day, the Paris Motor Show is still considered the largest auto show of its kind in the world, and each year it displays new and more impressive and technically advanced vehicles.

One of them, the Amilcar, was introduced in 1920, two decades after the first exhibition. The roots of the Amilcar, though, go back to 1909, when a man named Jules Salomon, a formally trained mechanic, went to work for Georges Richard, an electric car manufacturer. Salomon wanted to make his own car but needed funding and ideas. Through Richard he met a man who could help: Jacques Bizet.

Bizet had wealthy connections including a French banking family, the Rothschilds, who financed the early vehicles. Some reports have the Bizets related to the Rothschilds. Regardless, Jacques Bizet wanted to be associated with the history of motored vehicles, and the Rothschilds had the money to do it.

Thus, the Le Zèbre was born.

Judged by name alone, a car called Le Zèbre might perhaps resemble a zebra with black and white racing stripes. This was not so. Le Zèbre was a nickname given to a clerk at Richard's company. Reasons why this person was given such a nickname or why the car was named after him remain a mystery. But the Le Zèbre, or in this instance a series of car models, beginning with the Le Zèbre Type A, had an identification and soon built a reputation. It was also economically priced at 10,500 francs, about a thousand francs less than the nearest competitors.

The previously mentioned Amilcar resulted from Le Zèbre's success. Jules Salomon had as much to do with the Amilcar as he did with the Le Zèbre, this time with a man named Edward Moyet. Two other men, Emile Aker and Joseph Lamy created the Amilcar company. The name is said to be a somewhat loose anagram of Aker and Lamy. The Amilcar had a low, torpedo-shaped body, much like Le Zèbre, with a long nose extending out from the two open seats closer to the back and almost directly over the back wheels. Several models were made over the years including a racing version that featured a super-charged camshaft and a six- rather than a four-cylinder engine. It won many races.

"Once an Amilcar, Always an Amilcar," remarked author Gilles Fournier about the sporty vehicle's owner loyalty.

Jacques Bizet did not have any vesting interest in Amilcar, at least not directly. He had other ideas. Along with Georges Richard, Salomon's original employer, Bizet founded Unic, a pseudo taxi service, catering to those who needed long rides across France's countryside in something presumably faster than a carriage. One of Unic's best customers was Bizet's friend Marcel Proust, who would take long taxi rides along the coastline to Normandy, a setting that proved inspirational for many of his stories.

When the Amilcar was featured in the 1920 Paris Motor Show, it drew attention. Not only was it a carbon copy of Le Zèbre, but like its predecessor it was affordable. Thus in the echelon of French car history, the Amilcar had its place as did Le Zèbre before it. Jacques Bizet has something to do with that. However, something more dubious follows the Amilcar even to this day. Whether it shares any of the blame or warrants such a place in history doesn't really matter.

Amilcar is forever linked to the tragic death of Isadora Duncan.

3

Your mother wrote
me a letter

⟜ Even for someone as independent as Kathleen Scott, the restrained attitude she displayed over her husband's death came as a surprise to most Londoners. She simply did not want or expect any sympathy directed her way. Though circumstances at sea prevented the widow of Captain Scott from attending the memorial service in his honor, when she returned to London in April of 1913, a grieving nation was ready to embrace her. Kathleen wanted none of it. The only time she purposefully made a public appearance, as noted in the papers, was to go see Teddy Evans at the Charing Cross train station and offer her condolences for the loss of his wife Hilda.

However, Kathleen did not act as though Scott's death was unimportant to her or to the country. She accepted reparations from the British Admiralty, including Scott's pension, and was awarded the rank title she would have received had Scott returned and been knighted by the king as planned: Lady Scott. None of this was a bother except when others felt congratulations were in order. She mentions a brush with the British royal family in July of that year, shortly after returning from New Zealand, when she and Peter were invited to Buckingham Palace to meet Alexandria, the Queen consort. She wrote briefly that they "stayed an hour" and "[the Queen] photographed them together."

J. M. Barrie playing Neverland with Michael Llewelyn Davies. Wikimedia Commons, public domain [August 1, 1906].

Soon after, Kathleen left London bound for Andorra by way of Paris. "I very certainly must have more rest if I'm going to preserve my reason," she wrote. It was during this time that a response arrived from Barrie about the letter she sent him from Scott. "I have been hoping all this time that there was such a letter for me from your husband," Barrie wrote, "and the joy of which I receive it is far greater than the pain. I am very proud of the wishes expressed in it." Barrie then shared his desire to look after Kathleen and her son. "I know a hundred things he would like for me to do for Peter, and I want out of love for his father to do them all. And I want to be such a friend to you as he wished. I should have wanted to be that had there been no such letter, and now I feel I have the right to ask you to give me that chance."

Kathleen liked Barrie and took joy in knowing Scott would be pleased by their continuing friendship. She had seen how Barrie embraced the five Llewelyn Davies boys after the death of their father and admired him for that, but she was fine with Peter having a loving godfather and nothing more.

Around the same time, Barrie was being charmed by another Peter. A year earlier Barrie had received an anonymous letter at his home that contained a drawing of Peter Pan obviously done by a child. Inside the letter was a handwritten note from an unnamed woman explaining the drawing was done by her four-year-old son. The boy had written his full name on the drawing as Peter Lewis. Using the postmark and last name, Barrie tracked him down. He wrote Peter back:

"Your mother wrote me a letter but she did not tell me her name (which makes me like her better…), but she sent me some fine pictures u drew about P. Pan, and they are all just like the pictures P. P. would draw himself."

Barrie found out that Peter Lewis's godfather was someone whom he admired, another writer named George Meredith. It was just enough of a connection to justify Barrie continuing the correspondence. In time he got to know the family, including Peter's mother and Peter's three sisters—a contrast to Barrie's connection to the Llewelyn Davies family and its boys. Peter and his sisters were all about the same ages as the Llewelyn Davies boys, and Barrie thought they could play together.

Barrie and Peter Llewelyn Davies visited Cardiff, Wales, where the Lewises lived. He so enjoyed their retreat that Barrie agreed to return with more of the boys. The next visit, Barrie brought Michael and Nico, the two youngest of the five Llewelyn Davies boys. Michael, who was fifteen at the time, especially liked playing with the girls. "They are so utterly a family out of a book," he wrote to Mary Hodgson, the boy's nanny back home.

Many years later, one of the Lewis girls, Medina, recalled the visits from Barrie and the boys. "He [Barrie] was nervous to give the boys the pleasure; but after the visit he told my mother how much they enjoyed it, and even Michael 'the dour and impenetrable' (I distinctly remember those adjectives) said he wanted to come again."

Medina Lewis remembered Barrie watching them all play on the lawn and telling her mother: "They're so innocent, it almost hurts."

4

He was too frightened

Before she met Kathleen Scott, Isadora Duncan turned to Mary Desti for solace and guidance. The two were inseparable after meeting in 1901 when Desti left Chicago and arrived in Paris with baby in tow looking for a career as a stage actress. Desti was always there for Isadora and never wavered in her support. Along with a man named Gaston Calmette, the editor of *Le Figaro,* France's daily conservative newspaper, Desti organized the funeral arrangements for the children, including Isadora's insistence that the children's bodies be cremated—something generally frowned upon by French authorities. Isadora had made it clear to Calmette that she did not want the children "in the earth devoured by worms." Desti believed Isadora would stay with her after the funeral and get some rest, but Isadora had other plans.

When the press found out she was leaving Paris, speculation ran rampant. "As soon as she has recovered from the shock," the *London Times* reported, "she will devote the rest of her life to the care of the poor and sick…it is said she will leave for the field of operations in the Balkans and join the Bulgarian Red Cross." Before leaving Paris, Isadora issued a statement to the city: "My friends have helped me to realize what alone could comfort me," she wrote. "All men are my brothers, all women are my sisters, and all little children on earth are my children." Then she left and no one was quite sure if they would ever see Isadora in public again.

While Isadora contemplated how—or even if—she would return to performing, her relationship with Singer suffered. He was devastated by the loss of both children and was there for her at the funeral, but when she confronted him about having another baby, Singer told her it was "frivolous and inappropriate" to bring it up. He left abruptly, as he often did. Isadora knew this time it was probably for good.

Then Isadora suffered another loss: Gaston Calmette, her newspaper editor friend who helped Desti with the funeral arrangements for Deirdre and Patrick, was dead. Calmette was brazenly shot and killed by the wife of Joseph Caillaux, France's minister of finance, a staunch socialist who was strongly against France entering war with Germany. Calmette thought Caillaux's pacifist views were dangerously treasonous and used his newspaper to initiate a plan to remove him. Unbeknownst to Calmette, however, Caillaux's wife Henriette was planning something far worse. On March 14, 1914, while Calmette sat in his newspaper office, Henriette went to see him unannounced. Secretly, she was carrying a Browning revolver. "Do you not recognize me?" she coolly asked Calmette before pumping five bullets into his chest. When the police arrived, they found Henriette still holding the smoking gun. *"Je suis une dame!"* she told them. "I am a lady. Don't touch me."

When Isadora heard of Calmette's murder, she denounced it in a broader sense. "An uncanny pause seemed to hang over the land," she wrote. "It was a tragic event, the forerunner of a greater tragedy."

Isadora went to Rome to settle her mind. There she met yet another man, a handsome young Italian sculptor whom she knew through Rodin's studio classes. Romano Romanelli was his name and they took long walks together on the beach.

Several months later, Isadora felt a change in her body. She was pregnant. The expected baby was a revelation, like a "mythical dream," she remembered, that Deirdre or Patrick was being reincarnated. Romanelli was already engaged to another woman and immediately broke it off with Isadora, leaving behind a bust

Isadora Duncan and the Isadorables. The Library of Congress, part of the Genthe Collection.

he sculpted of her while they were still together. To cope, Isadora started to think about dancing again. Her plan was to bring the Paris dance school back to full capacity after the baby was born and eventually perform with her students again. She needed more funding, so she went to the one man who could provide it: Singer. She told him of the pregnancy. He hid his face in his hands, she recalled; then as he always did, he gave her the money she requested.

In June of 1914, Isadora's new pupils held their first dance recital. Isadora sat out of view of the audience and watched as her Isadorables danced to the music of Schubert in a tribute to Deirdre and Patrick. The crowd expected Isadora to make an appearance, but they were disappointed. Now visibly showing, she kept her pregnancy hidden. Less than two months later, on August 3, Germany declared war on France. Paris was transformed. Military uniforms were handed out in the streets. Curfews were enforced and the theater houses closed in anticipation of the night raids sure to come.

During all this chaos, Isadora went into labor. Just getting to a doctor was a chore in a time of war. Many of the streets were blockaded by guards, and Isadora and Desti drove from clinic to clinic in search of someone, anyone, who could take them. They found a reputable doctor in Bellevue who brought a nurse to help with the delivery. The doctor kept telling Isadora to "have courage, Madame," and the nurse seemed upset, as if something was wrong. The baby was delivered. *A boy!* Isadora held him in her hands and felt "gloriously happy and borne up to the Heavens with the transcendental joy of again holding my own child in my arms." Her joy only lasted a few hours. "Despite everything science could do," wrote Desti, "his little lungs would not expand." Isadora never gave her son a name. She blamed his death on the war.

"He was too frightened," she later said.

Several months later, on November 24, Isadora went to America. Many of her students in Paris and London were German nationals and Singer thought it was best to send them all to the United States for safety. Upon arrival, they were treated like immigrants—which in fact many of her students were—and detained for a time at Ellis Island. Still, Isadora felt like this was the new beginning for which she had hoped.

Isadora was comforted by friends, including actress Ellen Terry, Edward Craig's mother, and a group of artists and writers who met in Greenwich Village. There they discussed art and politics, mostly taking a socialist stance, like in Russia, which appealed to their creative and free-spirited sensibilities. "She is so marvelous… so beautiful, so kind. She was like a great Lovely Goddess Angel to me," Isadora wrote about Terry, the grandmother to her late daughter Deirdre.

Born into a theatrical family, Ellen Terry knew mostly actors and artists growing up. She became a child actress at age nine and at sixteen married the painter George Frederick Watts, thirty years her senior. Despite the significant age difference, she devoted herself to him, giving up acting to become his wife and exclusive model. The marriage was rocky and in less than a year, Terry returned both to her family and to acting, now famously known as the girl in Watts's paintings. Her return to acting, however, was short-lived. She met another man, an architect named Edward William Godwin. The couple had two children together even though Terry was still legally married to Watts. After divorcing Watts, she married an actor named Charles Kelly and made another return to the stage, this time in Shakespeare's *The Merchant of Venice* at the Prince of Wales Theatre. There she caught the watchful eye of Henry Irving, London's most popular actor and owner of the Lyceum Theatre. Terry was a rising star when she met Irving. She became the number one female lead in his company at the Lyceum (and perhaps his lover, too, although she disputed this). Nevertheless, they were London's most popular stage couple, doing mostly Shakespearian plays to adoring audiences in both England and in America.

Craig was Terry's son by Godwin. The name change reflected their concern for his illegitimacy. When Isadora met Craig, she gushed over his mother: "Ellen Terry, my most perfect ideal of a woman," she told him. Now in her sixties, Terry was still doing plays and touring as Shakespeare's heroines even though Irving, her stage partner for nearly twenty years, had died of a stroke in 1905.

On December 3, the Isadorables appeared at Carnegie Hall without Isadora. Then in January 1915, she made a grand return. "Miss Duncan seems to have experienced a change of faith as to the purely artistic purpose of her performances," Henry Taylor Parker, the HTP of the *Boston Evening Transcript,* described.

It only got worse from there. Isadora and her students danced to the music of Schubert's "Ave Maria" in two versions—one with Isadora dancing alone and the other with the Isadorables portraying angels circling about her. In between, the performance featured readings from the Bible and other literary sources with religious themes. "It is the most disheartening and amateurish mixture of music and recited literature, from the bible and other sources entirely unsuited for this purpose," HTP wrote. Another critic went even further: "Her failure was not due to lack of talent, but rather to an unconscious over-indulgence of egotism."

If the critics didn't understand Isadora's work at least Ellen Terry did. She collectively formed the "Committee for the Furtherance of Isadora's Work in America," and set out to put Isadora in touch with more appreciative audiences. The committee also helped promote the dancing school. Isadora was emboldened by the gesture. In February she danced at the Met and was greeted warmly. In a speech, she denounced the U.S. government for not entering the war in a time of great need and lambasted America's rich as "cold" and "heartless." She got standing ovations. In her last performance at the Met, she told the crowd, "I'm going to an island in the Greek Archipelago to live on bread and onions and worship beauty."

"What good is there left in America [for artists]," she added, "but the ships to take them to lands where their efforts are appreciated." For the next several months, as the spring flowers bloomed, Isadora appeared at the Century Theatre in Central Park West with a sixty-five-piece orchestra and a choir of nearly two hundred singers. She danced solo and appeared in acts of Greek tragedies. The Century run ended successfully in April. By May, Isadora was ready to return to Europe.

Ellen Terry on board the steamer *New York*. The Library of Congress, part of the Bain Collection [May 2, 1915].

Ellen Terry was going back to London as well. She invited Isadora and her students to join her on the ship *New York*. Terry also contacted her friend the actress Rita Jolivet, who was planning to travel along with Charles Frohman on another ship, the *Lusitania*. Terry told her that the *New York,* being an American ship, was likely safer to travel than the *Lusitania,* a British vessel.

Jolivet politely declined Terry's offer.

5

Not as of any moment

✍️ Although not directly traveling with Frohman, Rita Jolivet had booked a cabin on the superliner *Lusitania* in order to see her brother in England who was shipping out to the Western Front. Jolivet was twenty-five and one of Frohman's rising stars. She had appeared in several Shakespeare plays on London stages and was gearing up for more silent film work. Frohman took her under his wing like he had with Maude Adams and Pauline Chase, his two Peter Pans. He thought Jolivet, who had just wrapped up a film by director Cecil DeMille, had a chance to rival Adams in stardom.

Rita was thrilled to find others she knew on the *Lusitania,* including her brother-in-law George Vernon, the playwright Justin Forman, and fellow actress Josephine Brandell. Most fashionably dressed, Brandell and Jolivet made for a striking pair on the ship, certainly gathering admirers' attention during the evening dinners and concerts.

Shortly before Charles Frohman boarded the *Lusitania,* John Barrymore, the actor, tried to dissuade his friend from traveling on the British ship. Frohman shrugged it off. Barrymore then contacted Ethel, an actress herself who knew Frohman personally and the big sister to both John and Lionel Barrymore. Perhaps she could persuade him not to go.

"Ethel, they don't want me to go on this boat," Frohman told her.

"Yes. It's much against everybody's wishes," she replied.

He thanked her, kissed her on the cheek, and said everything would be fine.

When Frohman arrived at Pier 54 on May 1, 1915, reporters were waiting to ask him the obvious question. "Aren't you afraid of U-boats?"

In typical Frohman style, he wittily replied, "No I am only afraid of IOUs."

Despite the shrug off, there was cause for concern. The war was on in Europe, and British-owned ships were prone to attacks by German submarines. Just a month before, on March 28, the British liner *Falaba* was torpedoed by the Germans off the Irish coast killing 104 of the 242 people on board, including one American. The United States immediately warned citizens that traveling to England should be avoided unless they had "urgent business" to attend. Frohman felt he had urgent business. His friend James Barrie had asked him to sail to England as soon as possible to help fix a struggling play. Frohman did not hesitate. That's why without reservation he booked the largest and fastest liner across the Atlantic. Many others also ignored the warnings. Surely the Germans wouldn't be so brazen as to attack a ship filled with American passengers.

Don't be so sure, warned the German Embassy in Washington, D.C. On April 22, just days before the *Lusitania* would set off, they posted an ominous ad in the New York papers that read:

> TRAVELERS *intending to embark on the Atlantic voyage are reminded that a state of war exits between Germany and her allies and Great Britain and her allies; that the zone of war includes the waters adjacent to the British Isles; that, in accordance with formal notice given by the Imperial German Government, vessels flying the flag of Great Britain, or any of her allies, are liable to destruction in those waters and that travelers sailing in the war zone on ships of Great Britain or her allies do so at their own risk.*

Many paid only a passing thought to the Germans' threat. Others dismissed it as propaganda. The *Lusitania* was built as safe as they come, they were told. In addition, the British Admiralty would send an escort once the ship reached the war zone. What they didn't know was this: in Berlin, German military leaders were preparing a top-secret intelligence report listing all the merchant ships moving across open water that could be potential targets.

At the top of that list was the *Lusitania*.

On board the *Lusitania,* Charles Frohman would find a slew of associates with whom to confer, including Alfred Gwynne Vanderbilt who occupied the *Lusitania's* most expensive "Parlor Suite" that went for over $1,000 American dollars per night. Frohman and Vanderbilt had traveled together before and often spent time in each other's suites, smoking and drinking away the hours at sea. Another familiar face to Frohman was his friend from the Savoy Hotel, George Kessler. There was a good reason Kessler was on board. Business demanded he travel to England. Besides, just getting there was just as profitable for the "Champagne King": the larger ships like the *Lusitania* were filled with people who had money to spend. Kessler's presence on any ship insured that there would be plenty of Moët wine to drink. Frohman immediately seized on the opportunity and invited friends to his stateroom for a party, courtesy of Kessler and him, of course.

The trip was certainly not business as usual for the captain of the *Lusitania,* William Thomas Turner, who had received a communique of "special instructions" from the British Admiralty as to how to proceed through the so-called "submarine zone." Turner was so surprised at the sheer volume of instructions that he joked he could "paper the walls with them." The *Lusitania's* four tunnels, normally the standard black in color, were painted a more inconspicuous gray. Turner was ordered not to fly any flags. In addition, the portholes were to remain closed, bulkhead doors locked, and extra crew assigned to watch duty. The engine room was to maintain full steam power and be prepared to go even higher if instructed.

By law, the *Lusitania* also carried a sufficient number of lifeboats, twenty-two in all, to accommodate every passenger on the ship. This important change was made after the *Titanic* disaster, when there had been far too few. The wooden boats, eleven to a

side, stood "range down," meaning they were upright and ready
to drop when full. There were also twenty-six collapsible lifeboats
with wooden bottoms and canvas sides. In theory, the boats could
carry in excess of 2,500 people.

The number of lifeboats was just part of the overall safety pro-
tocols. Every morning at eleven, a crew of ten men would perform a lifeboat drill. At a whistle signal, they climbed into a sus-
pended boat, hoisted the oars, and sat. Then they would stand up
again, return the oars, and climb back on the deck. Watching all
this closely was George Kessler. Unlike others who put warnings
of an attack out of mind, Kessler had taken the threats seriously
and was keeping a close watch on the proceedings of the passengers and crew. One morning Kessler witnessed the morning lifeboat drill but was unimpressed. He approached the ship's purser,
a man named James McCubbin, and asked, "It's all right drill-
ing your crew, but why don't you drill the passengers?" Kessler
thought the passengers should know how to properly put on and
adjust life jackets. Even better, shouldn't all passengers be assigned
particular lifeboats so they would know where to go? The purser
brushed off Kessler's question and referred him to Captain Turner.

Captain Turner was a busy man but still found time to meet
with Kessler to discuss the matter. The two men stood and smoked
along the deck rail as Kessler reiterated his concerns. "I suggested passengers should be given tickets with a number denoting the
number of boats they should make [be available]," Kessler relayed.
"It seemed to me this detail would minimize the difficulties in the
event of trouble." Turner told him the issue had come up after
the *Titanic* disaster, but the Cunard line thought it was imprac-
tical. Plus, he had no authority to issue such an order...only the
Admiralty could. Then Kessler asked him directly his thoughts on
the possibility of a German attack.

The captain's response was short and direct.

"Not as of any moment," he said.

6

Their poor dirty pockets

୧୨ When war began in the summer of 1914, Kathleen Scott was in southeast England in Sandwich, Kent, with her son Peter. That year she had completed a commissioned bust of the *Titanic's* Captain Smith. Standing larger than life, Kathleen's depiction of Smith portrays the doomed captain in his naval uniform with his arms crossed and right leg forward, bending at the knee. Kathleen attended the unveiling ceremony in Lichfield's Beacon Park, then decided to put her sculpting work on hold and instead focus her time on the war effort.

She went to France as Lady Scott and used her title and notoriety for the common good. She sought out four English sisters who were trying to start a hospital staffed by British volunteers. In November 1914, Kathleen heard the sisters had chosen a hotel as a site, only to have it snatched up by the British military for other purposes. Kathleen vowed to help them find another location. The temporary hospital would soon find a home in a large, English-style chateau in Haute-Marne.

Kathleen took her influence even further. She met with the French war minister Alexandre Millerand whom she found surprisingly accessible. Kathleen told Millerand that since the hospital's location had been moved it was now eleven miles from the

Statue of Captain Edward Smith by Lady Kathleen Scott in Beacon Park, Litchfield, Staffordshire, U.K. Creative Commons [photograph 2010].

nearest train station. She insisted he provide mobile ambulances for transport. Millerand granted her wishes.

Kathleen convinced other British artists and writers to help, including poet Laurence Binyon, whose time at the hospital would inspire his most famous work, "For the Fallen," a poem recited at Remembrance Day ceremonies in Great Britain to this day.

They shall grow not old, as we that are left grow old.
Age shall not weary them, nor the years condemn.
At the going down of the sun and in the morning
We will remember them.

In January 1915, Kathleen bravely tended to wounded soldiers at the hospital by emptying their pockets of any belongings and labeling their clothes and boots for fumigation. "So pathetic and characteristic were the contents of their poor dirty pockets...oh so dirty...mud and blood and dust...and such a smell," she wrote. But the work was personally rewarding. "I can't bear them to be just numbers. I always feel ashamed when I have to refer to them as numbers." She found pictures of wives and children on their person. One red-haired fellow hit in the jaw and delirious, she described, "had a three-year-old boy."

When she returned to London, Kathleen began working on a factory line in Vickers making electrical coils. The work was laborious and gritty, but she enjoyed the camaraderie with the other women. Many had husbands, boyfriends, even fathers who were fighting on the front lines. Kathleen was thirty-five and a widow. But what if Scott had lived? Certainly, he too would be fulfilling his duties in the Royal Navy. So Kathleen tried to keep up the girls' spirits by entertaining them and keeping their minds off the war. She treated them to participation activities during lunch breaks; in the evenings they went out together to dance the foxtrot. In her diary, she mentions taking forty girls to see *Peter Pan*. "Oh how ludicrously happy one is in this sad, grim world," she intoned.

While Kathleen was giving of herself for the better good of the country, Isadora was returning to Europe after the successful run in New York. Her on-again-off-again relationship with Paris Singer was, well, off again. After the death of their son Patrick,

Singer was mostly out of Isadora's life. He did, however, continue to support her work financially. When she needed money to help fund the dancing school, he was there. He even bought some land and promised to build a school in her name. After Britain declared war on Germany, he looked after her safety as well. Singer sent Isadora and her students to the United States so they could continue to dance without the distractions. Before they all left for America, however, he told her of one thing he was especially proud: the transformation of his family's Oldway House in Paignton into a military hospital. He even donated $25,000 for supplies.

Isadora approved. She had supported England's and France's entries in the war but felt contempt for her fellow Americans' indifference so far. When she traveled to Naples in May of 1915, she remarked: "Thank God for your beautiful country and don't envy America (Italy had just entered the war). Here in your wonderful blue skies and olive trees, you are richer than any American millionaires."

In retrospect, the comment might have been misconstrued as insensitive. Many American millionaires, including one of its richest, had left New York shortly before Isadora did, bound for Liverpool.

They were on the *Lusitania*.

7

The ship can't sink

⚜ Indeed, one of the richest men in America was aboard the *Lusitania,* Alfred Gwynne Vanderbilt. At the age of thirty-seven, Vanderbilt, tall and handsome, was the heir to a family fortune begun with his great-grandfather's shipping and railroad fortune. Known as "the Commodore," Cornelius Vanderbilt cut his teeth in transportation on the Hudson River and Long Island Sound before owning the most successful rail lines in New York. When he died in 1889, his children became rich as did their children eventually. This included Alfred's father, also named Cornelius.

An avid horseman, Vanderbilt was traveling to London to attend the International Horse Show Association. He was accompanied by his private secretary, Charles Williamson, who brought along the actress Amelia Baker with him. Baker was in Charles Frohman's repertory but hadn't enjoyed the successes of some of his other actresses. Still, she was on her way to Paris to make her stage debut there.

Thanks to his uncontrolled spending, by 1915 Vanderbilt's forty-two-million-dollar net worth had been cut nearly in half. Still he was wealthier than most Americans and thanks to his name, a very well-known and recognizable man. As one person astutely described, of all the *Lusitania* passengers, "There were one or two bankers [on board], and a Vanderbilt."

Alfred Gwynne Vanderbilt. The Library of Congress, part of the prints and
photographs division, Alman & Co. N.Y. [1906].

During the trip, Charles Frohman hosted a lavish party in his suite. Frohman stayed mostly secluded since the ship set off, but this was a chance to mingle in the comfort of his own quarters. Frohman had been nursing a right knee injury suffered during a fall at his home in New York, but not until he started using a cane did others know something was wrong. Those close to Frohman knew he kept most of his private life private. In one brief display of frankness, however, when asked why he never married, Frohman explained, "I could never have taken the risks that as a theatrical manager I am constantly called upon to do." It might be said that Frohman's closest relationship was with a man, another lifelong bachelor and a playwright, Charles Dillingham, with whom he shared a home in White Plains, New York. The two were dearest friends, and the press, too shy back then to venture into more provocative insinuations, left "the two Charlies" mostly alone.

Everyone Frohman knew was invited to his party including Vanderbilt, the actresses Rita Jolivet and Josephine Brandell, and the American author Elbert Hubbard, who ironically had penned the first book about the *Titanic* disaster in 1912 just months after its sinking.

Hubbard, outspoken and strangely boyish with his trademark Stetson hat, long coat, and Buster-Brown-style haircut, may have been the most-talked-about figure in the room. Frohman was so equitable in his invitations he even invited the ship's barber to come. For his part, the barber named Lott Gadd remembered that evening when "Mr. Hubbard came in and we chatted about ships being sunk by torpedoes."

As the ship was getting closer to the Irish coastline, the uneasiness in the room was apparent. Those who bore no reservations while boarding were understandably more nervous now. Josephine Brandell was one. She attended Frohman's party and asked another passenger, Mabel Crichton, if she could sleep in her cabin that night so as not to be alone. She hardly got any sleep, she recalled. Later Brandell and Crichton would lunch together.

George Kessler also had a restless night. When morning broke, he went out to the deck rail to have a smoke. There he met Edgar Gorer, a London art dealer. Talk revolved around the relative merits

of sighting a British escort ship once the early morning fog lifted. While the sight of an escort ship might settle nerves, any merchant or passenger liner with an armed escort would still not be
protected from attack under maritime law. They might be better
off without it; then again, they might not. British destroyers had
been sent before, even once escorting the *Lusitania* safely to shore,
but on this day no escort ship would arrive.

After lunch, many of the passengers took to the deck rail to
watch the fog burn off. The beautiful Irish coast was waiting. It
would be the first time in six days they would see anything other
than choppy seawater.

"There, there it is there, it's Ireland," someone said.

Everyone shaded their eyes and looked ahead.

Then someone shouted "Look, there's a torpedo!"

Earlier, Vanderbilt, Kessler, and Frohman were in Vanderbilt's
suite discussing the war. Vanderbilt hoped to do some good for
a change by spending his money on the allied cause. "They have
disgraced themselves," he told Kessler about the Germans, "and
never in our time will they not be looked upon by any human being
valuing his honor save with a feeling of contempt."

There are varying reports regarding exactly where each of the
three men was located on Friday, May 7, at 2:10 P.M. when a torpedo struck the ship, but afterward they all found each other on
the deck rail, discussing what to do next. Frohman was seen on the
upper promenade deck with Rita Jolivet's brother-in-law George
Vernon and another man Alick Scott, an English captain in the
Royal Navy. When Jolivet, Vanderbilt, and Kessler joined him,
Frohman was casually smoking a cigar, apparently unfazed by the
events at hand. "I didn't think they would do it," he said.

Passengers who heard the explosion streamed to the deck rails
for instructions. Others hoped to return to their cabins to rescue
possessions. Most remember the mad scramble to get or find life
jackets. "She's alright," someone was heard shouting, "she [the
ship] will float for an hour." Many grabbed life jackets from their
cabins and waited by the lifeboats to board. One observer noted
that they came with their life jackets haphazardly worn or only

Captain William Thomas Turner. The Library of Congress, part of the Bain Collection [1915].

holding them in their hands as if they weren't needed yet. In the meantime, the boat was listing. Too soon, many thought. "We are sinking rapidly," one passenger told his wife. "It cannot be long now."

Inevitably, the ship's power went out. This led to even more confusion. Those leaving their rooms found hallways and stairways completely dark. In the bowels of the ship where food was stored, electric elevators were jammed. Workers there were trapped. The blackout also temporarily shut down the wireless radio transmission until a backup storage battery revived it.

There were plenty of lifeboats, both wooden and collapsible, but no plan as to how to get them safely in the water. Despite the engines being down, the *Lusitania* still managed a good headway, perhaps too fast to launch the boats. Moreover, she was listing nearly thirty degrees to the starboard side. Passengers were helped one by one into the hanging boats, but just as soon as they were seated, an order came directly from Captain Turner. "Don't lower the boats!" he shouted over and over, fearing for their safety. "The ship can't sink. She's all right. The ship can't sink." Turner, seen wearing his life vest, then asked some able men to help him get the women and children out of the boats.

None of this seemed to bother Frohman. According to Jolivet he kept smoking and carrying on a conversation as if it were just a normal day. He was, however, concerned about Jolivet. "Save your strength," he said calmly, implying she might need to hang on to the rail. The bow was so far forward that the propellers and rudders were sticking out of the water in back.

Despite the captain's orders not to board the lifeboats, many still did, thinking they might provide the only recourse when the boat finally did sink. There were also twenty-six collapsible boats, but they were tied down. In some instances, many thought they were glued to the deck so as not to slide off. Even the crew members had a difficult time releasing them. One woman with a baby was thrown off her feet as the boat lurched forward. A man arrived to help her. "Don't cry," he said, "it's alright." It was Alfred Vanderbilt. She recognized him. He looked around for a spare life jacket but found none. He gave up his instead. She climbed into a boat and waited. Another eyewitness described seeing Vanderbilt helping other women and children put on life jackets.

George Kessler had witnessed the torpedo striking the ship, which looked like "a snakelike churn of the surface," he thought. It was followed by a "thud." At first, he didn't know what had happened. Some believed the ship had struck a mine. Few believed it could be a torpedo strike. Kessler soon found Frohman and Rita Jolivet. They were all handed life jackets. Jolivet helped put one on Frohman, but he just as quickly took it off and gave it away. "Don't bother about me," he told her. None of them decided to search for a lifeboat. It was too late. Instead, they waited together, held hands, and braced for the worst. Jolivet remembers Frohman turning to her and smiling.

"Why fear death?" he said. "To me, it is the most beautiful adventure in life."

Just then a swell of water parted them all.

8

The most beautiful adventure in life

✍ When news that the *Lusitania* had sunk was broadcast on May 8, 1915, Kathleen Scott could not help but think about her friend Isadora. When the first dispatches of the tragedy hit the streets, Isadora Duncan was rumored to be one of the many prominent figures on the ship. Kathleen had already got confirmation that Charles Frohman had been aboard. Thinking Isadora may have traveled with him, Kathleen feared the worse for Isadora. Soon she would learn that the famous dancer had traveled back to Europe aboard another vessel and had arrived safely in Italy. Kathleen did not know Mr. Frohman personally, but as Barrie's friend she shared his anxiety as dispatches arrived daily from the Irish coastline on who was lost, who was found, and who had survived the *Lusitania* attack.

At the same time in London, Barrie was working on a revue he had written for Gaby Deslys whom he was grooming to make a legitimate star. Deslys needed no help in being popular, especially with men. But in working with Barrie, she found something she had not received so far: credibility and respect. Their partnership was both curious and titillating. "The astonishing fact of the matter is that it's a *personal* friendship," wrote the appropriately named British society magazine the *Tatler.*

When word got out that they were working on something together, it was the talk of London. The night *Rosy Rapture* opened on March 22, 1915, at the Duke of York's Theatre it was easily the most anticipated theater event of the year. The house was packed. Then the show began. It was uneven, quirky, and altogether different. "If not for the name on the playbill and some mechanical jokes on stage, we would have never detected Sir James's hand in this revue," wrote the *London Times*. Deslys took the brunt of the barbs. "If you are more attracted than repelled by her," the *Times* added, "you will be more pleased than bored by *Rosy Rapture.*"

Barrie would not admit to another failure. Over the next several weeks he called for more rehearsals and made cuts and alterations in an attempt to salvage his project for Deslys. But the nightly receipts, while not overtly disappointing, still yielded empty seats. Then on May 8 the news arrived with a headline in the *Guardian:*

"THE *LUSITANIA* TORPEDOED. LOSS OF SEVERAL HUNDRED LIVES FEARED."

The newspaper reports conveyed that of the 1,900 passengers on board, "500 to 600" passengers had been saved. More would be known within days. Barrie awaited word. A few days later, he would get it: Charles Frohman was no longer missing. Several ships, including one named the *Bluebell,* had picked up survivors and dispatched them to Queenstown, the closest port to the disaster site. Bodies that were either put on a ship or washed ashore were then placed in rows on the streets. Charles Frohman was one of these. It is said Captain Turner, who was rescued in the water, was the first to recognize him. A "most beautiful and peaceful smile" was still on Frohman's face, the *London Times* reported.

Rita Jolivet somehow survived. When she was thrown off the railing by the surge of rushing water her boots ripped off her feet. Her hand, once clasped to Frohman's, let go. In the water she grabbed a collapsible lifeboat filled with passengers and clung to its side until another lifeboat passed and she climbed in. When she got to Queenstown, she searched in vain for her brother-in-law George Vernon, only to discover he had been lost. She also found out about Frohman. Three years later, by her own admission, Jolivet would relive the nightmare in a movie titled *Lest We Forget.* The end of the film includes a dramatization of the *Lusita-*

Charles Frohman shown here reported to be on the *Lusitania*. New York Public Library, part of the Billy Rose Theatre Division [1915].

nia disaster with Jolivet re-creating scenes from real life, including her encounter on the deck rail with Charles Frohman.

Frohman was once asked about how he would like to be remembered. "All I ask is this," he said, "he gave *Peter Pan* to the world." Even a Barrie biographer admits that while it was Barrie's imagination and words that brought the boy Peter to life, "had it not been for Frohman's daring and vision, there would have been no *Peter Pan.*" Frohman's faith in Barrie extended to a deep mutual respect. They understood each other, and, in the end, thanks to Jolivet's publicized story, Barrie could take solace in his friend's final words: "Why fear death? It is the most beautiful adventure in life."

The line was similar to one from *Peter Pan*. At the end of the mermaid's lagoon scene, Wendy and Peter are trapped on a rock as the lagoon's water is rising. "Soon the water will be over it," Peter tells her. Peter is wounded and cannot fly so he ties Wendy to a kite string hoping she will lift off to safety. Wendy demands Peter tie himself to the string as well. "It can't lift two," Peter explains. Wendy then asks Peter to draw lots. "And you a lady," Peter retorts angrily, "never!" Peter lets the kite string go. "To die will be an awfully big adventure," he explains as Wendy floats up and away.

How exactly Charles Frohman worded the line after "why fear death" is recounted in several ways, but Rita Jolivet remembers it as "it is the most beautiful adventure in life." Upon hearing the news, Barrie wrote to Pauline Chase. "I feel sure that his last words were really, 'To die will be an awfully big adventure,' just like in *Peter Pan"* and left it at that.

9

There is much we cannot see

ᴄ∕◯ "The Champagne King" George Kessler survived. After spending some time with Frohman and Alfred Vanderbilt on the deck rail, Kessler said he went forward toward the captain's bridge and started to help some of the women into a lifeboat when the *Lusitania* listed, and he was thrown in with the others. The boat was lowered. "Scarcely had we gotten the boat clear of the falls when the Lusitania disappeared," he told reporters. "It was too sudden to describe. It just happened. Immediately there was a tremendous suction and the boat overturned." The lifeboat was pulled under by the suction. "How far I went and how long I remained underwater I cannot tell," Kessler added. "It seemed a lifetime." Kessler finally came to the surface. The boat and his companions were gone. "I swam almost involuntarily, how long I do not know, and finally found a collapsible." The collapsible was filled with nine men; eight of them were the ship's strokers. "Big, husky, young fellows," Kessler described. They were all desperately trying to empty the boat of water. "We tried bailing and balancing, but the boat would tilt and turn and finally capsize again."

Despite their efforts, the boat would right itself then "turn turtle again," Kessler explained. After numerous attempts the boat was finally upright, but the physical exertion took its toll. When the *Bluebird* picked them up, six of the strokers were dead. There were reports that as many as nine bodies were found in the boat face down in the water. Kessler was not one of them. "How I stood the three-hour struggle is more than I can understand," he would later say. When he arrived in Queenstown with the others, Kessler was besieged by reporters asking about the missing, specifically Alfred Vanderbilt. "I am certain he perished," Kessler told them.

Others would tell the tale of Vanderbilt's final minutes. One account was truly courageous. Shortly after the torpedo struck, Vanderbilt was spotted outside the Palm Saloon doors talking to a servant. "Find all the kiddies you can and bring them here," he told the man. Vanderbilt then grabbed two children, one under each arm, and hurried them off to a lifeboat. He did this several times until all the children in his care were safe. Then as one report goes, he began to help the women. When the ship sank, Vanderbilt, like Frohman, went with it. Unlike Frohman, however, his body was never recovered.

Justus Miles Forman, who had written *The Hyphen* and was traveling to London at the request of Frohman, was another unfortunate victim. His body was also lost to the sea. At forty-one, Forman was younger than Frohman by seventeen years.

A fellow playwright on board was Charles Klein, a colleague of Frohman's, who in 1915 had just missed being on the *Titanic* thanks to a business meeting that was delayed. Later he expressed how "horrible" it must have been for the passengers of the *Titanic* to have "no escape" and "wait for death helplessly." After hearing Frohman and Forman were going abroad on the *Lusitania,* Klein, who lived in America but was English-born and preferred to write in England, hurriedly booked passage on the ship to discuss his latest project with Frohman. "A run across the Atlantic to attend to business, to greet old friends, to renew old friendships, and then...the hideous bolt of doom on the *Lusitania,*" was how the newspaper dispatches described Klein's fate. Whether his body was ever retrieved is debatable. A man named James Brooks, a weed chain salesman from Maine who survived the attack, claimed he found and identified Klein's body by his clubfoot. Klein's name, however, did not appear on the recovery list.

Another story being told concerned the American author Elbert

Elbert Hubbard on the *Lusitania*. The Library of Congress, part of the Bain
Collection [1915].

Hubbard, who knew a little something about shipwrecks. His book about the *Titanic* disaster, the first to be published, was a best seller. Now Hubbard was traveling to Europe in hopes of scoring an interview with Kaiser Wilhelm after writing a scathing article about the German monarchy titled "Who Lifted the Lid of Hell?" Hubbard hoped to get Wilhelm's response to the accusations. Along with his wife, Alice, Hubbard booked a cabin on the *Lusitania*. Charles Lauriat, a survivor, was with the Hubbards when the torpedo struck. He told them he was leaving to go to his stateroom to get a life belt. "Hubbard stayed by the rail, affectionately holding his arm around his wife's waist," Lauriat told reporters. "Both seemed unable to act." When Lauriat returned, the Hubbards were gone. Several passengers picked up the story after Lauriat left. The Hubbards were seen holding hands then walking casually up the grand staircase, presumably back to their room. They were never seen on the ship's decks again. Their bodies were never found.

Actress Josephine Brandell was another survivor. She fell into the water after boarding a lifeboat that quickly capsized. She hung onto a floating deck chair until help arrived. "The cries for mercy, the people drowning and coming up again and barely touching me was too terrible," she later described. Her friend and lunchmate, Mabel Crichton wasn't so lucky. She was missing for nearly a week until her body was eventually discovered.

Like the many who survived to tell their stories, Kessler's harrowing ordeal changed his life. While he was bailing water in the collapsible, Kessler made a promise to use his influence and money to help victims of the war. After recovering from his injuries, Kessler set out to find a cause he could support. He visited hospitals throughout London and talked to soldiers injured by war. One such hospital was likely the estate in Paignton, Paris Singer's transformed Oldway residence, now called the American Women's War Relief Hospital and run by a group of American-born English women. Its main benefactor was Britain's Lady Randolph Churchill, the mother of Winston, who was born Jennie Spencer in Cobble Hill, New York. Any records of Kessler's visits at other hospitals throughout England are overshadowed, however, by the one in which he found his calling: St. Dunstan's, a country house on seventeen acres in the middle of London.

Kessler's visit to St. Dunstan was prompted by meeting Sir Arthur Pearson. A former newspaperman, Pearson had gradually lost his eyesight to glaucoma and now devoted his time and efforts to helping those with severe eye disorders. As one author put it, "He [Pearson] was the blind man whose job it was to look after other blind men."

When the war broke out, Pearson heard that a Belgian soldier had been visually impaired in battle and was being treated at a London hospital. Instead of sympathy, Pearson encouraged the boy to be positive about the future. When two more soldiers were reported with debilitating eye injuries, Pearson gave them the same sage advice. "He at once resolved that some plan must be devised to give the men who had lost their sight in the war a new start to life when they were discharged from the hospital," wrote biographer Sydney Dark.

Pearson went even further: he opened a hostel for blinded soldiers. At first, there were only five residents, but that would soon change. Pearson went to work teaching them how to lead useful lives, despite their disabilities, just as he had done. He invited friends and influencers to visit and talk to the men, hoping to instill a confidence that inspired independence and productivity rather than self-pity. Dark describes one day when the nursemaid approached Pearson and told him one of the men was despondent. "Despondent? What on earth does he have to be despondent about?" Pearson said. Pearson then approached the man and explained, "There is much we cannot see and there is one thing we will not see if we can help it, and that is the gloomy side of our lives."

In March 1915, two months before the *Lusitania* was attacked, Pearson had moved his hostel from a small room on Bayswater Road to a house in Regent Park near Piccadilly Circus. He promptly dubbed the organization St. Dunstan after a former church on Fleet Street named for the tenth century bishop and known for its large projecting clock. Pearson promptly bought the clock and put it outside his building.

Most of the larger hospitals in town were requisitioned to serve

Sir Arthur Pearson at the Red Cross Institute for the Blind N.Y.C. The Library of Congress, part of the Bain Collection [1915-1920].

as military facilities, including St. Thomas near the Charing Cross station, where many of the severely injured or maimed soldiers were sent. This is where an actor named Herbert Marshall spent thirteen weeks recovering from a bullet wound to the knee that refused to heal. Marshall was working when war broke out in Europe, touring in America with an English cast in a show called *Grumpy* when Parliament changed its conscription law to include all English men eighteen to forty-four, single or otherwise, for recruitment. Marshall was newly married but that no longer mattered. The cast returned to England and Marshall at the age of twenty-four enlisted in the British Army. A year later he was in the hospital, his left leg so badly infected that doctors ordered it removed, and he was fitted with a prosthesis. When King George V came to visit, Marshall stood up wearing trousers and asked his highness to choose which one of the legs he thought was fake. The king chose the wrong one.

These are the kind of stories George Kessler was hearing when he sought out a cause in which to invest his time and money. That's when he found Pearson visiting the ward at the 2nd London General, where soldiers with eye injuries went. Kessler was moved by what he saw. Pearson gave every soldier he visited a specially made watch with hands that were slightly raised and dots for numbers. He called it the Pearson watch. "A blind man always wants to know the time," he told the men and invited each one to join him at St. Dunstan when their hospital stay ended.

Inspired by the work at St. Dunstan's, Kessler along with his wife Cora Parsons spent $50,000 to set up the B.F.B. (British, French, and Belgian) Permanent Relief War Fund. Sir Arthur Pearson would head up the British chapter. In 1915, the fund's office opened in Paris, and a year later Kessler started a similar operation in New York City known as the Permanent Blind Relief War Fund for Soldiers and Sailors of the Allies. One of its original trustees was a thirty-eight-year-old deaf and blind woman Kessler knew.

Her name was Helen Keller.

LEFT TO RIGHT: Mrs. Cora Parsons-Kessler, George Kessler, Sgt. Major Robert Middlemiss, Mrs. John H. Macy, Mrs. R Valentine and seated Helen Keller at the B.F.B. Permanent Blind Relief Fund Headquarters, N.Y.C. Perkins School for the Blind clippings, World War I [1916].

10

The public is never wrong

⌒◡ Maude Adams, Frohman's most acclaimed actress, was in Kansas City on a multi-city tour of a Barrie play titled *The Ladies Shakespeare* when she received a telegram from Frohman's office in New York. "The *Lusitania* has been sunk by a German submarine," it read. "Charles Frohman is presumed dead."

For the *Peter Pan* actress, the death of her friend and mentor was devastating. She cried hysterically and told the theater's staff to cancel that night's performance only to be informed that the banks were closed and no refunds could be offered. Under the circumstances, she graciously obliged their wishes to continue. With puffy eyes and voice cracking, she carried on. The audience apparently was not informed about Frohman's fate until after the show.

Even though Frohman's funeral was in New York City, Adams organized a memorial service for him in Los Angeles, strangely enough, at the Mason Opera House. Frohman showed little interest in the West Coast and rarely if ever traveled there. However, his actors did. They spoke glowingly about the man who flat out made their careers. The funeral was attended by mostly entertainment-types and included several songs from Frohman productions. Adams was too distraught to attend.

Adams, like other actors from the New York stage, was in Los Angeles because the industry demanded it. Theater productions previously written and designed for the stage were now being redone and adapted for film. Los Angeles and specifically Hollywood were at the heart of the film productions. Frohman resisted at first. "Transferring plays to screen is a ridiculous and quixotic dream," he once told Adolph Zukor, head of Paramount Pictures. "The medium [silent movies] is so different and the players would worry about that. They depend on their voices, which on screen would be useless."

Zukor, however, was persuasive and the public demand for entertainment was changing. Before the *Lusitania* disaster, feature-length films like *The Birth of a Nation* were packing in audiences at New York movie houses, and Frohman's Empire Theatre attendance was beginning to suffer because of it. Frohman agreed to sell rights to his plays, but only reluctantly. "The public is never wrong," Zukor would tell Frohman, who was still not convinced. As it turned out, he would never live to see his actors ascend to even more greatness on the silver screen.

One man who could envision the ineluctable impact of the burgeoning film industry was producer Jesse L. Lasky. Lasky worked closely with Zukor and was just as instrumental in the success of Paramount Pictures. He was also a clever promoter whose creative vision culminated on October 19, 1915, when a Hollywood silent movie actress named Anita King pulled into Times Square in New York City and became the first woman on record to drive a touring vehicle solo across America.

King had broken no speed record—the trip had taken forty-eight days—but was she really trying? Lasky and Paramount Studios sought publicity for the stunt and publicity is exactly what they got. The papers were all over it. "Colorful, convoluted, and contradictory" is how one writer described King's elaborate and perhaps embellished tales from the road.

King was no stranger to adversity. She was born to immigrant parents who settled in Michigan City, Indiana. Her father committed suicide in 1896 when she was twelve. Only two years after that, her mother succumbed to tuberculosis, leaving King a grief-stricken teenager and an orphan. She moved from Michigan City to Chicago where she found work as a model and actress. In 1908

Anita King in the Kissel Kar, from the private collection of Lucianne Board-man, courtesy of Lucianne Boardman.

at the age of twenty-four, she traveled to California where she be-came fascinated with motor vehicles. She competed in a few auto races but after an accident decided to concentrate on her acting career instead. She appeared in a couple of comedic films, but they were merely bit parts and nothing star making.

That's when Lasky started thinking about the Lincoln Highway, the newly opened coast-to-coast route between San Francisco and New York City that ran through thirteen states. Although it was dedicated in 1913, the road was still a work in progress. Lasky said that it would be at least ten years before the highway would be in such shape that a "lady" could make the drive without difficulty.

King chimed in. She alone could drive a car and make the trip right now. Seeing the promotional value in the stunt, Lasky was immediately on board and agreed to pay for it. For transportation he secured a major sponsorship with the Kissel Motor Car Com-pany, which furnished a machine built for endurance and adver-tised as "every inch a car" and an "all-year vehicle." King's job was to act like a "movie star." In return, Lasky promised, he would make her one.

Dubbed "the Paramount Girl" by the papers, King drove the Kissel Kar with a "new set of Firestone tires"–another Lasky spon-sor. "There will be nobody with her," the *Los Angeles Times* report-ed, "her only companions will be a rifle and a six-shooter." The trip began appropriately in front of Lasky's Paramount studios in Hollywood.

Greeting well-wishers along the way, King made stops at over a hundred Paramount theaters. But for most of the three-thousand-plus-mile journey in between, the infectious thirty-year-old still had to drive long stretches by herself over paved and unpaved roads and in all types of weather. There were other challenges to be met as well. In the Sierra Mountains, she recalled, a "tramp" tried to hitch a ride. "I wouldn't permit myself to show how fright-ened I was," King said. "I handed him a flask of whiskey I had in the car and told him to come to the theater where I was appear-ing the next night." He did, according to King, bringing a bouquet of picked flowers with him.

Each story King told reporters seemed to be more extraordinary than the last. In a harrowing incident just outside of Reno, King's tires became stuck in the mud. She spent hours trying to shovel them out to no avail. Then suddenly, she was not alone: a "mad coyote" joined her company. "Gee it looked as big as a house," she explained. "I finally killed him and knew nothing more until I was picked up by prospectors who heard the shots of my gun."

When she arrived in New York City, King was the guest of honor at a ceremonial dinner and shook hands with dignitaries. In typical fashion, though, the city's newspapers, while celebratory, were skeptical too. "Miss King, in spite of being on the road from September 1 to yesterday, had no marks of tan or sunburn," the *New York Sun* pointed out. King explained she used grease paint on her face all the time. "I was determined I wouldn't come into New York City with a red nose," she said.

King became a celebrity darling and a movie titled *The Race* starring King and Victor Moore went immediately into production. It was released the following year. Much to Lasky's disappointment, the film garnered poor reviews and ran for only a week. King's exploits on the road, though hailed in the papers, apparently weren't as interesting re-created.

King, however, had fond memories of the groundbreaking trip. Later in an interview, she recalled meeting a young girl on the side of the road who had packed a bag and wanted to run away with King to the movies. Recalling her own sad upbringing, King gave her some heartfelt advice: "I would give the world to have what you have right there in that home," she said. Then King got back in her car, waved goodbye to the little girl, and drove off to her next adventure.

The stunt ended only a few months after the *Lusitania* disaster, so if Lasky's intention had been to replace anxiety with hope, it worked for a time. The prospect of the United States entering the European conflict, however, would eventually bear down on the country. Still for one shining moment in New York City, home of the theater district and Broadway Street, which made Charles Frohman famous, there was a new darling in town, a silent movie actress from the West Coast named Anita King.

11

Oh, the poor things

⫷ In London, James Barrie had to make a difficult decision. *Rosy Rapture* with Gaby Deslys was faltering and the man he had called upon to save it was now tragically gone. As one writer described it, the loss of Charles Frohman was "the death knell for *Rosy Rapture.*" After the *Lusitania* disaster, Barrie lost all interest in the play and immediately shut it down. Deslys took it in stride. Barrie never held her responsible for its failure and later collaborated with Deslys in adapting parts of the revue for use on her traveling tour. Beyond that, they did little else together.

In the meantime, while Frohman's funeral was being held in New York City, Barrie took on the dubious task of planning the annual Christmas production of *Peter Pan,* now a tribute to the man who helped bring it to stage so successfully. Barrie made some changes. He decided to drop the lagoon scene, partly due to budget constraints, but as some suggest, perhaps because he could not bear to hear Peter say the line: "To die will be an awfully big adventure." That year, he also began work on a new play.

Even with the war escalating and the *Lusitania* sinking still reverberating, Kathleen Scott still had no reservations sailing the coastline. Only once when a boat she had traveled on was sunk two weeks later by the Germans, did she entertain "grim thoughts." They did not stop her. She traveled to Paris and Rome before reaching Carrara to begin work on Scott's statue, then returned to London in 1916. There she made it a point to visit her friend Isadora Duncan.

Isadora was in a bit of a freefall. She had avoided being on the *Lusitania* and for that she could be thankful, though some thought it had more to do with lack of funds than with luck. In truth she had planned to go to Italy all along instead of London. The part about being financially unstable, however, still had some merit to it: Singer's money was running out.

Isadora found herself back in Paris and strangely alone. To help with the war effort, she invited hundreds of soldiers, senators, and French government ministers to the house she rented on Avenue de Messine to party continuously with "food and wine." Many of the young soldiers had put their careers as painters and musicians on hold to fight. "Oh, the poor things, they are artists," Isadora would explain. "And they were so hungry. It was the least that I could do." To help offset the costs and pay off the debts, Isadora planned to dance again in Paris. It would be the first time she would perform there since the loss of her children.

At some point in 1916, Isadora was back in London to meet with Kathleen. Only Kathleen recalls the visit in her diary. Isadora had gained weight, Kathleen noticed, and was drinking more. She was also "playing games," as Kathleen described it, cavorting with different men, several per week, many of them married. Kathleen certainly didn't need Isadora's blatant sexual exploits to reassure her that something might be missing in her own life.

During the strains of war, Kathleen spent some of her most lighthearted moments with James Barrie who was still pressing her for partial guardianship of Peter. Kathleen could tell that Barrie was still affected by Scott's death. Only the letter Scott wrote to him from the Antarctic offered some comfort.

Despite the personal losses and professional disappointments, Barrie was bouncing back. In 1915, after the failure of *Rosy Rapture,* Barrie kept busy working on that year's production of *Peter Pan* while writing a new play titled *A Kiss for Cinderella,* a wartime fantasy that debuted in March of 1916 at Frohman's Duke of York's Theatre. Barrie's story involves a servant girl named Miss Thing (the Cinderella of the play), who takes care of refugee chil-

Auguste Rodin. The Library of Congress, part of the prints and photographs
division, Gertrude Käsebier, photographer [1905].

dren left homeless by the current war. One day she is greeted by
a woman in a nurse's outfit who grants the girl three wishes. The
first wish is to go to the Royal Ball. The second is to help the war
wounded, and the third is to marry her prince charming, a police-
man who at one point helps save poor "Cinderella's" life. In the
end, everyone lives happily ever after. *A Kiss for Cinderella* was a
needed hit for Barrie and ran for 156 performances. Later that
year, it opened on Broadway and starred Maude Adams.

While mostly isolated in London and Paris, Isadora grew frustrated by the lack of support and empathy she was receiving over
her financial situation. "Still not a word from anyone," she wrote
referring specifically to Singer and her brother Augustin. *"Please*
write me news." From Singer she was looking for money, something he always seemed to provide when she asked. "If you could
persuade Paris [Singer] to cable money, it would be a salvation,"
she wrote Mary Desti.

Isadora went to New York to see friends and seek out Singer who
finally responded to her request and agreed to provide funding to
help save the dancing schools. When she arrived back in America, however, many of her students had left. Then Singer surprised
her by holding a benefit concert at the Met. Isadora was overjoyed
to dance at the prestigious concert hall again. "One of the most
beautiful experiences of my life." The following year, Singer officially divorced his estranged wife and married a nurse named Joan
Balsh who worked at the American Women's Hospital run from
Singer's Oldway mansion in Paignton. Singer had been secretly
having an affair with Balsh since 1912.

At the end of 1917, Isadora grieved over the death of sculptor
Auguste Rodin, the man who brought her and Kathleen together. "It is difficult to think of Paris without Rodin," Isadora told
friends. "But Paris will never be without Rodin...his spirit is there."

Kathleen would be just as distraught, but more introspective.
"I am very humbled as a sculptor," she wrote, referring to his influence. Kathleen and Isadora would share in the moment but spend
little time together after that.

Their lives taking wholly separate paths.

12

How I like these Americans!

⌒◯ Although Captain Scott had told Kathleen in his last letter that had he no reservations of her remarrying, Kathleen's relationships with men after her husband's death were mostly platonic. One man who intrigued her, though, was the American diplomat Colonel Edward M. House, President Woodrow Wilson's right-hand man and most trusted advisor. Texas-born and raised, House wasn't a colonel, per se. It was only an honorary title. He never served in any war. But as a Texan he knew about guns and attitudes. He also knew how to intimidate and win fights. Despite this, he was also sympathetic and kind to his closest confidantes. Even his political foes found him tough but endearing. "An intimate man even when he was cutting your throat," is how one adversary's son described him.

Kathleen and House met in New York in 1913, and now that escalations included the U.S. involvement overseas, Kathleen couldn't help but be more interested in what he had to say. When the conflict ends, House explained to her, there may be glaring differences in perspectives and attitudes on how to envision a postwar Europe.

That prophecy would come true in 1919 when the heads of the four allied superpowers, now known as the "peacemakers," met in a conference in Paris to draw up a new global map based on the

Colonel Edward M. House. The Library of Congress, part of the Bain Collection [1910-1920].

war's impact. The treaty signed in Paris known as the Treaty of Versailles was historic, and the subsequent months of talks that led to its agreements were contentious at best.

Within all of it, one person shone through: not a politician, not even a man, but a queen. Like most people outside of southeastern Europe, Kathleen didn't know her personally, but she enjoyed hearing stories about the formidable Marie, the Queen Consort of Romania.

Born into royalty in 1875 as Princess of Edinburgh in Kent, England, Marie Alexandra Victoria rose to the title of Queen Consort when her husband Ferdinand, a third cousin of Marie's became the heir presumptive to the Romanian throne in 1916.

Marie was a different kind of queen, less submissive and daringly independent. During the start of war, she spent time with the Red Cross in hospitals risking her own life in the disease-filled tents. Although she was British-born, Marie had great respect for the Romanian people and would venture into the countryside unaccompanied by guards. Many villagers crowded her, kissed her hands, and fell down at her feet. "At first it was difficult unblushingly to accept such homage," Marie wrote, "but little by little I got accustomed to these loyal manifestations. Half humbled, half proud, I would advance amongst them, happy to be in their midst."

In contrast to Marie's adventurist spirit, the king was far less dynamic. Quiet and shy, Ferdinand's most enduring feature was his ears, which stuck out the sides of his head like a teddy bear. He said little and mattered even less. Marie, however, was the complete opposite. Pretty and intelligent, she spoke out when asked and possessed a seemingly good knowledge of foreign affairs. When the war ended, Marie was the more vocal one, not her husband.

It seemed only fitting then that in the summer of 1919, Ferdinand sent Marie to attend the Paris Peace Conference. The glamorous Marie did more than just attend. She hobnobbed with the press, flirted with world leaders, and, although she had an important job to do for her country, found time to go on lavish shopping sprees with her three daughters.

Instead of being intimidated at the conference as might be ex-

pected, Marie intimidated others with her saucy manners and
salty speech. In one instance, she invited herself to lunch with U.S.
President Woodrow Wilson and his entourage and then showed
up fashionably late with an entourage of her own in tow. "I could
see from the cut of the president's jaw," one guest noted, "that a
slice of Romania was being lopped off."

According to reports, Marie dominated the conversation. "I have
never heard a lady talk about such things," remarked Wilson's
traveling doctor. "I honestly did not know where to look, I was so
embarrassed."

It all paid off. Romania grew in size and population. In fact, of
all the contributors at the conference, Romania is widely considered to have picked up the greatest gains, including Transylvania
which became and remains a part of "Greater Romania."

"I had given my country a living face," Marie said about her visit
–clearly an understatement.

One person who was impressed with the Romanian queen was
Kathleen's friend Colonel House. "She is one of the most delightful personalities of all the royal women I have met in the West,"
he gushed about Marie.

Before the conference though, and thanks to House's candor,
Kathleen became more interested in the intricate workings of the
war. She and House would meet in Paris while he was visiting various heads of state as Wilson's representative. They drove the coastline together and talked about peace after wartime. She was especially interested in hearing his description of the proposed League
of Nations. Kathleen remembers him telling her: "if it [League of
Nations] goes through it will be more important than the Magna
Carta, the Declaration of Independence, or anything."

House disclosed to her things he could never tell the president,
like policy disagreements that would boil over during the peace
talks. Katheen found it all thrilling and informative. "How I like
these Americans!" she described in her diary.

In November of 1918, the war was over. Kathleen met with Barrie to celebrate the Armistice signed on the eleventh day of that

Queen Marie of Romania. The Library of Congress, part of the Bain Collection [1920-1925].

eleventh month. They giddily joined in the revelry. "Jimmy [Barrie] came after six and we played together until midnight," she wrote. "After dinner we went out together arm in arm to watch the delirious crowd playing 'kiss the ring' on the Grand Boulevards—mad, wild scenes...girls dressed as widows were dancing with the rest."

For Barrie the end of the war came as a welcome relief. He mourned the senseless deaths of Charles Frohman and the others who perished on the *Lusitania,* and he had grieved like a father when the eldest Llewelyn Davies boy, George, was killed in action. Barrie, however, also had reasons to be thankful. Peter Llewelyn Davies, at nineteen, went to the Western Front in 1916 where he survived the fierce Battle of the Somme. He was sent home a few months later suffering from eczema and shell shock and never went back. Then Michael, the second youngest of the Llewelyn Davies brothers, was set to enlist on November 12, 1918, the day after the ceasefire agreement was signed. "I don't think the army needs him now," Barrie wrote to an acquaintance about Michael's good fortune. "You can guess how thankful I am."

13

I write a word
of farewell

Isadora Duncan spent the postwar years with a man named Walter Morse Rummel, a pianist, composer, collaborator, and, as one writer described in relation to Isadora, her "lover of record." He had a calming influence. For one, he was recently divorced and able to devote all his time to her. Professionally they worked together, giving joint recitals to packed crowds. Isadora was thankful for a steady presence in her life. "I believed that this was the only one for whom I waited so long," she wrote, "that this love would be the resurrection of my life."

It would not be.

When Isadora and the Isadorables reunited in Paris, Rummel, who at thirty-three was ten years younger than Isadora, began to fall for one of the dancers, a snappy twenty-three-year-old named Anna Denzler. Isadora confronted the obvious by immersing herself into work. In Greece, she met her old friend the photographer Edward Steichen, who filmed her in various stages of dance. One particularly striking photo has Isadora in the Parthenon extending her arms as if reaching for the heavens.

Kathleen, for her part, found herself inundated with requests to sculpt war memorials, plaques, and bust of war heroes. It kept her thinking and busy. Along the way, many men charmed her but never moved her enough to consider marriage. She always found a

Mrs. Hilton Young (Lady Scott). The Library of Congress, part of the Bain
Collection [1920-1925].

way out, convincing herself, in often frivolous ways ("fat, dull, and egotistic"), why each one was unworthy. Then she met Edward Hilton Young. "He's the most exciting personality," she wrote shortly after they were introduced. "I think I adore him."

Like Scott, Hilton Young was a navy man and had served admirably in the war. Early on, he lost an arm in a battle while serving as an officer on the HMS *Vindictive*. Later in 1919, he volunteered for the British expeditionary force in the Russian civil war. In between, Hilton Young dabbled in politics and served as a minister of Parliament for Norwich. According to friends, they met amongst a crowd at Kathleen's studio. "I'm going to marry that man," one acquaintance claims Kathleen said to her after spying Young from afar. Hilton Young had a past, including a relationship with Virginia Stephen. He had proposed to her, but she refused him. Virginia Stephen would go on to become better known as Virginia Woolf, one of Britain's most famous modernist writers of the twentieth century.

Kathleen fondly remembered being happy during this time. Peter was twelve and the constant calls she had received about Scott, either questions or approbations, were finally ending. "These marvelous, peaceful days are inexplicable," she wrote. "Scarcely anyone comes, scarcely anyone rings up. It is really perfectly lovely. I can't account for it, but may it endure!" Then she got some shocking news from Isadora about their mutual friend Edward Steichen. Ever since Kathleen met Steichen at that small café in Montparnasse some twenty years earlier, things began to change for the young artist. Steichen encouraged her to open up. He insisted she meet the great sculptor Rodin, which led to meeting Isadora. Now Steichen was in her life again, but she wished it was for better reasons.

Steichen was on a roll professionally. Not only were his photographs and paintings as popular as ever, he was also working feverishly to set up exhibitions for other artists. These included a showing of Rodin's bronzes and works by the Society of Younger Painters in Paris, a group he organized in 1908. His personal life, however, was not as successful. Steichen's wife of twenty years,

Clara Smith, was filing for divorce, and both Isadora's and Kathleen's names were being mentioned as possible reasons. It was all silliness to Kathleen, who while close to Steichen never "lived together or anything of the kind," she explained.

Kathleen admitted she and Steichen spent a week together back in England, but it was "idyllic and platonic." Another story had Kathleen meeting Clara just to diffuse any jealousy. "Never ask me to do that again," she reportedly told Steichen afterward.

The possibility Steichen had an affair with Isadora was more plausible. By that time, Isadora's reputation for promiscuity was well established. Isadora spent more time with Steichen than Kathleen did, and his provocative photographs of her at the Parthenon and in more personal settings and in various stages of undress likely set Clara off.

Accusations aside, the disparaging rumors coming out of New York made Kathleen uneasy and angry. This might have changed her mind on commitment. She began seeing Hilton Young again, exclusively. It took several years, but in January 1922, he asked her if she would be his wife. "How absurd," Kathleen wrote about the proposal in her own personal way, but she said yes.

On March 3, 1922, Kathleen and Hilton Young were married in the Crypt Chapel of the House of Commons. It was a private affair with only Peter by her side. The ceremony took ten minutes. The couple took a short honeymoon to Wiltshire, before motoring back to London so Hilton Young could get back to work. The next few weeks were filled with conferences, art shows, and her husband's official dinners. For Kathleen, being the wife of a British minister was certainly different from being the widow of a revered explorer. She even made a "political" speech on his behalf. "It felt fine," she wrote about the speech, although as an artist, she felt clearly labored over the task.

Several months later, however, she was reminded again of Scott's influence.

In May 1922, James Barrie gave an address to graduating seniors at St. Andrews University in Scotland, where he had served as the appointed rector since 1919. Barrie looked frail and weak from

James M. Barrie at his rectorial induction. Courtesy of the University of St. Andrews Library, U.K. [May 3, 1922].

a nagging illness, but his speech was confident and moving, empowering students to have courage in the face of a changing world.

"I want you to take up this position," he told them. "Youth have for too long left exclusively in our hands the decisions in national matters that are more vital to them than us... Do not stand aloof, despising, disbelieving, but come in and help—insist on coming in and helping. After all, we have shown a good deal of courage, and your part is to add a greater courage to it. There are glorious years lying ahead of you if you choose to make them glorious."

Midway through the hour-long address, Barrie paused and reached into his breast pocket. "I should like to read to you some passages of a letter from a man of another calling, which I think might hearten you." Barrie held up a piece of paper. "I have the flimsy little sheets here," he described. "It is a letter to me from Captain Scott of the Antarctic and was written in the tent where it was found long afterward with his body and those of some other very gallant gentlemen, his comrades."

He read from it: "Hoping this letter may be found and sent to you, I write a word of farewell. I want you to think well of me and my end. We are in a desperate state, feet frozen, etc., no fuel, and a long way from food, but it would do your heart good to be in our tent, to hear our songs and our cheery conversation."

Barrie stopped and read over words in his mind before returning to the text. "Goodbye...I am not afraid of the end, but sad to miss many a simple pleasure which I had planned for the future in our long marches."

Barrie had never publicly released the letter in full, only parts. Even during the address, he seemed to gloss over the passages which he felt were too personal. Only after Barrie died from pneumonia in 1937 did some of the more intimate references come to light. Scott wrote: "I never met a man in my life whom I admired and loved more than you, but I never could show you how much your friendship meant to me–for you had much to give and I nothing. Goodbye my dear friend. Yours ever, R. Scott."

14

Isadora, your shawl

❧ In the spring of 1921, Isadora received a telegram from the Soviet government asking her to come to Moscow and dance. It read: "Only the Russian Government alone can understand you. Come to us, and we will make your school." Isadora responded: "Yes, I will come to Russia, and I will teach your children, on one condition—that you give me a studio and the wherewithal to work." The Soviets agreed. Isadora left for Russia leaving her "demons" behind, as she said. She pleaded to Mary Desti to come with her. "Of course, I realize that present conditions in the Soviet Union are difficult for a regime in the throes of stabilizing," she told Mary Desti, but her decision to go wasn't based on politics, it was based on art. "Life in Europe is too passé. It is too hopelessly bourgeois ever to understand what I am really after."

Desti went only as far as the ship's entranceway and wished Isadora well. "She thought she was on her way to Paradise," Mary would write later, "where all was perfect love, harmony, and comradeship."

Russia proved to be that at first, but it was a challenge. Now overrun by the Bolsheviks, postwar Moscow was wracked with crimes of communist oppression and terror. Still, Isadora was a legend, and the city embraced the arts and its artists, who kept mostly out of the political fray. Now middle-aged and slightly heavier, Isadora fed into the country's undeniably prudish sensibilities by dancing to Russian music and often times wearing red tunics or flowing red scarves. Enthusiastic and curious crowds packed the theaters to see her dance, and little girls by the hundreds flocked to her school. There were so many, Isadora recalled, she had to send many away in tears.

Isadora was no stranger to criticism, but the stinging rebukes of her performances from mostly male critics were hurtful. At one performance her "massive bare legs" and "wobbling breasts," as one writer described, fell out of her tunic. "Not a pretty sight," he wrote. Isadora could have left but decided to stay. Her plans, she told the press, were to remain in Russia for ten years.

In fall of 1921, only months after arriving, Isadora met a young Russian poet named Sergei Yesenin. They began a whirlwind romance that eventually led to Isadora accepting his hand in marriage the following year. The reaction was one of shock to her many admirers. "A wedding, a wedding," Isadora teased them, "for the first time in her life, Isadora has a lawful husband."

Yesenin was only twenty-four, blue-eyed and blond. Despite concerns from close friends, like Mary Desti, who warned her of trouble ahead, Isadora fell for him instantly. Yesenin was a heavy drinker and a womanizer and prone to bouts of alcoholic stupors, depression, and paranoia. "Isadora was never to know an hour of peace," Desti wrote, "and it was not long before she discovered her young poet was not only a great genius but also a mad one."

Isadora and Yesenin's subsequent years together were turbulent and destructive. He insulted her in public calling her "old." He trashed hotel rooms by breaking things—mostly doors and plate-glass windows—either by force or simply by falling into them. Yesenin promised many times that he would sober up but never did. The two broke it off several times.

Then in 1924, even though his marriage to Isadora was still binding, Yesenin married another woman, Sofia Tolstoy, the daughter of the Russian writer Leo Tolstoy, famous for his 1896 novel *War and Peace*. A year later the troubled poet slit both his wrists, wrote a "goodbye" poem in his own blood, and hanged himself from a heating pipe.

None of this appears in Isadora's memoirs. The book, entitled *My Life,* ends with her leaving for Russia in 1921, before meeting Yesenin. Isadora explained that the book would be banned in the United States if she wrote about her "communist years," which may have been true. She also may have been embarrassed by her own actions, especially in relation to the marriage, something for years she so strongly stood against. Speculation from others is that she just may have gotten tired of writing or, in this case, transcribing her life story. She had promised to write a second edition, though, in her own mind, most of it was still yet to be lived.

On September 14, 1927, shortly after the first typeset draft of the book was sent to New York, Isadora was at her studio in Nice, waiting patiently for a man she had met named Benoît Falchetto. Falchetto worked as a garage mechanic; she had consulted him about finding a car to purchase. He was to come to her studio at nine. At the time, Isadora was juggling several men in her life, including Singer, with whom she had recently reconciled.

Desti confided in Singer to help Isadora. He refused at first, but she begged him to come. After meeting Isadora in Paris, Singer agreed to send her a check. Desti asked her curiously if Singer was the one man Isadora truly loved. "I don't know, I seem to love each one of them to the uttermost limits of love," she told her. "I wouldn't know which one to choose. I loved, and still love, them all."

Falchetto was her latest catch. She was excited about taking a road excursion with the dashing mechanic and future race-car driver. Anticipating that he was bringing an open-wheel sportster, Isadora chose to wear a red shawl to keep off the chill. It was a gift from Desti who had brought it with her from New York. Isadora loved it. Nearly two-yards-long and five-feet-wide with a long, eighteen-inch fringe on both ends, Isadora could wrap it around her shoulder and neck several times. The warmth was comforting.

When Falchetto arrived, Isadora kissed Desti goodbye and strolled to the sporty Amilcar, a low two-seater known for its sleek, torpedo-shaped design and speed. Desti watched from the large studio windows as Isadora climbed in and adjusted the end of the shawl over the side of the door so it wouldn't blow in her face. *It's too long,* Desti thought. "Isadora, your shawl," she shouted over the engine's whine. "Pick up your shawl." But it was too late. As Falchetto sped off, the shawl's fringe caught the back wheel's spokes. Isadora never had a chance to react. The jerk hurled her violently out of her seat. Despite the gruesome details of the body being dragged for twenty to thirty meters before the car screeched to a halt, Isadora was dead from the moment the shawl tightened around her neck.

Isadora Duncan. The Library of Congress, part of the Genthe Collection.

Memory

⌒𝒪 At age fifty, Isadora was no longer the international sensation she had been in her youth, but her shocking and grisly death
made front-page news all over the world. Kathleen was in Geneva,
Switzerland, at the time with her husband, now a delegate of the
League of Nations. Peter was nineteen, and her other son, Wayland, was six. Wayland came a year after she married Hilton Young.
Kathleen did not mention Isadora's death in her diary. On September 15, the day after the horrific accident, Kathleen wrote of looking forward to leaving Geneva with Hilton for a weekend getaway.
That day she attended the circus with her children. "The tiger had
a fit," she described, "and the tension was awful." There was no
record of her being in Paris at Isadora's funeral, which according
to reports attracted thousands.

Since 1916, Kathleen felt Isadora's life was hurtling in a direction different from her own. Isadora was drinking more and care-
lessly carousing with multiple men. Kathleen maintained their
friendship mostly through correspondence. "I guess she wouldn't
have changed," she later reflected after Isadora's death, "and yet
there was a generous creature and an unsurpassed artist." The
only other time Kathleen mentioned Isadora in her diary was nearly ten years later. It was a place that spurred a memory.

In 1903, Kathleen traveled with Isadora to Greece. The two hardly knew each other, but Kathleen fondly remembered the famous
dancer being so moved by Greek culture that she bought a house
in Kopanos on Mount Hymettus. Isadora had hoped to dedicate
it to Hellenism, a place to worship the gods of the arts and dance
and sing and meditate from sunrise to sunset. Raymond Duncan,

Isadora's brother spent years renovating the building, but eventually left it abandoned when the money ran out.

In March of 1938, while in Athens, Kathleen asked to be taken there. She had heard it had been torn down, but she was wrong. "It was quite untouched, and half-roofed," she discovered. "The big wooden doors were locked, but I hammered and peeped [in]." Two Greek men with a goat greeted her warmly. One spoke French. The house was being used by the nearby refugees, he told her. They would come for miles to drink from its well and sleep in the grassy inner court or the "big room" that Kathleen remembered was now "inhabited by pigeons."

The man went on to explain that the house belonged to Isadora Duncan's father, "an elderly man who lives in Nice," he said. The thought of that, obviously not true, was rather amusing to Kathleen since they were likely speaking about Raymond. Either way, she thought, how fitting that Isadora's name still be attached to the old building, now being used to help those in need.

"It was to me a tremendous emotion." Kathleen wrote about that day. "It all came back. It all came back."

Today in Athens, there is an Isadora & Raymond Duncan Dance Research Center (DDRC) housed in the same historic building built by Isadora's brother Raymond in 1903. Founded in 1980, the Center is described as "an international residency center for individual artists and dance companies elaborating experimental and research projects." Currently, the Center is home to more than four hundred students—both children and adults. Many of the younger dancers still refer to themselves as "Isadorables."

Postscript

༄ **Isadora Duncan** was cremated at the Père Lachaise Cemetery on September 19, 1927. There were no funeral rites or eulogies. As with her performances, there was only music. The ceremony ended with the strains of Bach's "Air on the G String." Her ashes were then placed in a columbarium just below her children's.

Two years after Isadora's death, in 1929, **Mary Desti** wrote a lasting tribute to her friend titled *The Untold Story: The Life of Isadora Duncan 1921–1927*. In her own words, she detailed Isadora's life, as she was a witness to it, including the accident that killed her. Desti claims Isadora was in good spirits that day and was looking forward to the car ride. Desti, however, was nervous and shouted to Falchetto the driver, "I don't think you realize what a great person you are driving tonight. I beg of you to be careful. If she asks you to go fast, I beg of you do not." Falchetto replied, "Madame, you need have no fear, I've never had an accident in my life." Before the car sped off and ended Isadora's life in an instant, Desti writes that Isadora threw her hands up in the air and said these last words, *"Adieu, mes amis, je vais á la gloire!"* ("Goodbye my friends, I go to glory!") Eight years later in 1937, Desti died of leukemia at the age of seventy-one.

Preston Sturgis, Mary Desti's son, ended up having a successful career as a writer and director of many popular Hollywood movies in the 1930s and '40s, winning an Oscar for Best Original Screenplay in 1941 for *The Great McGinty.*

Before Isadora's death, **Paris Singer** had been spending most of his time in Palm Beach, Florida, the residence he established during the war. He invested nearly a quarter of a million dollars in Palm Beach buying up land and funding the construction of ten country villas that he donated to the U.S. government to aid wounded soldiers. These later became the popular Everglades Club. Singer spent his final days between Florida and Europe after losing most of his fortune when the stock market crashed in 1929. Two years later, he died of heart failure at a London Hotel. Singer is affectionately known as "the Father of Palm Beach" for having turned swampland into one of the largest concentrations of private wealth in the United States. Singer Island there is named for him.

After **Charles Frohman's** body was brought back to America, he was laid to rest at the Union Field Cemetery in New York City. It was not his final wish. Frohman had told friends that when the time came he wanted to be buried in a small churchyard in Marlow, England, a place "better than any in the world," he once said. The church sat near the cottage where Frohman spent lazy weekends with Pauline Chase. He even picked out a spot under a large willow tree. When Frohman's death came unexpectedly, however, his family chose otherwise. They insisted Charles's final resting place should be in the city where he began his career, near the theater and street that made him. Chase, though, did not forget Frohman's wish. She led an effort to help fund a memorial in Marlow. The stone monument, erected on Easter Sunday, April 20, 1924, depicts a nymph that, as the inscription reads, "symbolizes the spirit of youth, as portrayed in Frohman's most famous production." It still stands today at the foot of the Marlow Bridge, the main road leading into town, where no one can miss seeing it.

Five years after the sinking of the *Lusitania* in 1920, **George Kessler,** "the Champagne King," died from an enlarged liver. He was fifty-seven. After his death Cora Kessler, his wife, and Helen Keller continued to raise money and support training programs for soldiers blinded in the war. Thanks to Kessler's kindness and to the promise he made to himself during the *Lusitania* disaster, the original fund established in 1915 still remains in operation today as Helen Keller International.

Kathleen Scott's last diary entry was dated December 14, 1946. She was happy and enjoying her family. She was pleased that Peter, at age thirty-seven, had opened a bird reserve on the River Severn, his love for nature fulfilling his father's dying wishes. Earlier that year she recalled meeting with George Bernard Shaw, then ninety, and marveled at his dexterity. "His mind and gestures are as active as ever and his memory for what we had said and done thirty years ago quite prodigious." The next year, she was too weak to write; her heart was failing. She died peacefully at her English home on July 24, 1947, at the age of sixty-nine. "Here is what you shall put on my tiny gravestone," she told her husband several years before her death: "Kathleen. No happier woman ever lived." There is no marker or burial site. After a funeral service at the West Overton Church in Wiltshire, her body was cremated.

Peter Scott ended up turning his love for nature into a lifelong career. He became one of Great Britain's foremost conservationists of the twentieth century and helped found the organization World Wide Fund for Nature, still in existence today as the WWF. He served in the Royal Navy during World War II and died of a heart attack in 1989 shortly before his eightieth birthday.

George Bernard Shaw lived to be ninety-two, besting Kathleen Scott in age by nearly thirty years. He even outlived his most prolific pen pal **Mrs. Pat Campbell,** who died of complications from bronchitis in 1940 at age seventy-three. The so-called "love letters" the two exchanged were published in 1952 a year after Shaw's death.

Rita Jolivet, the actress who was the last person to see Charles Frohman alive never let the *Lusitania* sinking leave her memory. "How do you imagine it changed me?" she responded when asked that very same question. "No, you cannot imagine. And I cannot tell you how much it changed me. There are not any words." Thanks to *Lest We Forget,* the film she made depicting a scene from the *Lusitania,* and spearheaded by the Liberty Loan Drive, Jolivet launched a campaign to help sell war stamps. Armed with a bullhorn and in front of large crowds, she urged all Americans to follow the message of the movie and give: "I hope those who see it will never forget, at least not until we have wiped out all possibilities for such catastrophes in the future." At one such rally, over $18,000 in stamps were sold. Proceeds from Liberty Bond subscriptions where Jolivet spoke would eventually total in the hundreds of thousands. On March 2, 1971, at the age of eighty-one, Jolivet died of complications from surgery on a hip bone she broke while trying to dance the jig. "Oh, she would go like that," a friend remarked.

After appearing in James Barrie's *A Kiss for Cinderella* in 1925, **Maude Adams** ostensibly retired from the stage. She still sought out film roles although she never actually appeared in one. Instead, she worked behind the scenes with General Electric and Eastman Kodak in developing stronger stage lighting and the advancement of color photography, perhaps, as some have suggested, to make a color film version of *Peter Pan*. She never married. Instead, rumors of romantic trysts with the men she was professionally associated with like Frohman and Barrie would dog her career. In reality, for nearly fifty years, Adams maintained a close partnership with a woman named Louise Boynton. After Boynton died in 1951 at age eighty-five, Adams followed in July of 1953 at the age of eighty. They share a headstone together.

Pauline Chase retired from acting in 1913 after her seventeen-year-long run as Peter Pan ended. She made only one other public performance, this time for charity, in a 1916 film scripted by Barrie and presented to members of the British royal family. She married a wealthy English banker, had three children, and lived quietly in Kent, England, until her death in 1962 at the age of seventy-six.

James Barrie would know only sadness and heartbreak in the later years of his life. In 1922, only a few months after giving his speech to the graduating seniors at St. Andrews, Michael Llewelyn Davies, the second youngest of the five Llewelyn Davies boys, perished in a tragic drowning accident at Oxford. George Llewelyn Davies, the oldest of the five boys, had died in the war, but Michael's death, so sudden and senseless, was even more devastating for Barrie. "All the world is different to me now," he wrote. On June 19, 1937, after battling a long illness, Barrie at the age of seventy-three, fell into a sleep at his home on the West End of London and never woke up. "He was so tired," wrote Nico, the youngest Llewelyn Davies boy. In 1929, eight years before his death, Barrie gave the stage and screen rights to *Peter Pan* to the Great Ormond Street Hospital for Children in London. Thanks to the lasting legacy of "the boy who wouldn't grow up," the hospital, affectionately known today by its acronym GOSH, is still benefiting from Barrie's generous gift.

Gaby Deslys. The Library of Congress, part of the Bain Collection [1910-1915].

Barrie's last obsession, **Gaby Deslys,** whom he desperately tried to make a star with *Rosy Rapture,* never found the legitimate stardom he sought for her. However, her sex appeal and beauty were enough to make her quite popular and as it turns out quite wealthy, too. Her story, however, ends quickly. In December of 1919, only a few years after the disappointment of *Rosy Rapture,* Deslys felt a chill, then a fever, from which she never recovered. She died a few months later on February 11, 1920. Although she battled a chronic cough and throat issues, the suddenness of her illness and the rapid decline of her health were surprising. Unfortunately, it was not uncommon at the time. Many others experienced the same symptoms and the same outcome. Although records are spotty, it is widely suspected that millions died from the onslaught of the Spanish flu pandemic that began in 1918. Deslys is considered another victim of that deadly disease. She was thirty-eight.

Acknowledgments

I'm in gratitude to the team at Amika Press who helped make this book possible. Dr. Jay Amberg and John Manos for their honesty and direction, Mark Larson for his concise copyediting, Sarah Koz for guidance and professional design, Ann Wambach for precise proofreading, and Stephen Seddon for his thorough indexing.

To Mark and Sarah especially, whom I consider friends, a special thank you for making this book better beyond even my expectations. This latest project idea took many difficult and conflicting turns and could not have been completed without your influence, advice, and reasoned responses to my questions. The look of this book: the typesetting, chapter design, and photo framing is all due to Sarah's keen instinct and expert's touch. There truly is an art to book making!

A special gratefulness goes to my brother Mike Zurski, Randy Whalen, the late Christoph Traugott and my immediate family and in-laws, whom I reached out to and received encouragement and support along the way. I have a longer list of names, too many to include here, who will receive personal acknowledgements from me in its place.

To my radio fans, friends and work cohorts, including Greg Batton and Mike Wild, thanks for listening and understanding.

Finally, I offer infinite thanks to my children Sam and Nora, truly an inspiration, and my wife Connie whose unwavering support, determination and keen insights keep me grounded and focused every day. I love you all.

Bibliography

I'm indebted to the many librarians including the staff at my local library in Morton, Illinois, for providing materials and search options for the books you see listed here. In lieu of citations, I have embedded as much information about source materials as possible within the text. In cases in which no single direct origin can be attributed, the material is marked as originating in the source from which it was found.

Baatz, Simon. *The Girl on the Velvet Swing: Sex, Murder, and Madness at the Dawn of the Twentieth Century.* Mulholland Books/Little Brown & Co., 2018.

Birkin, Andrew. *J. M. Barrie and the Lost Boys: The Real Story Behind Peter Pan.* Constable and Company, 1979.

Bloom, Ken. *Broadway: An Encyclopedic Guide to the History, People and Places of Times Square.* New York: Facts on File Inc., 1991.

Cherry-Garrard, Apsley. *The Worst Journey in the World.* Penguin Books, first published by Constable and Company, 1922.

Curtiss, Mina. *Bizet and His World.* New York: Alfred A. Knopf, 1958.

Desti, Mary. *The Untold Story: The Life of Isadora Duncan 1921-1927.* New York: Horace Liveright, 1929.

Downer, Lesley. *Madame Sadayakko: The Geisha Who Bewitched the West.* Gotham Books, 2003.

Dugard, Martin. *The Explorers: A Story of Fearless Outcasts, Blundering Geniuses, and Impossible Success.* Simon & Schuster, 2014.

Duncan, Isadora. *My Life.* Boni & Liveright, Inc., 1927.

Everitt, Anthony. *The Rise of Athens: The Story of the World's Greatest Civilization.* New York: Random House LLC, 2016.

Frohman, Daniel and Isaac Frederick Marcosson. *Charles Frohman: Manager and Man.* Reprint Jefferson Publication, 2015.

Garden, Mary and Louis Biancolli. *Mary Garden's Story.* Simon & Schuster, Inc, 1951.

Gardiner, James. *Gaby Deslys: A Fatal Attraction.* London: Sidgwick & Jackson, 1986.

Kennet, Kathleen Bruce Young. *Self-Portrait of an Artist: From the Dairies and Memoirs of Lady Kennet (Kathleen Lady Scott)*. London: John Murray, 1949.

King, Greg and Penny Williams. *Lusitania: Triumph, Tragedy, and the End of the Edwardian Age*. New York: St. Martin's Press, 2015.

Kurth, Peter. *Isadora: A Sensational Life*. Little, Brown & Co., 1995.

Larson, Erik. *Dead Wake: The Last Crossing of the Lusitania*. New York: Crown Publishers, 2015.

MacMillan, Margaret. *Paris 1919: Six Months That Changed the World*. New York: Random House, 2001.

McWilliam, Rohan. *London's West End: Creating the Pleasure District, 1800–1914*, Oxford University Press, 2020.

Mérimée, Prosper. *Carmen: A Dual-Language Book (English-French)*. Print on demand, Amazon, 2022.

Miller, Julie. *Cry of Murder on Broadway: A Woman's Ruin and Revenge in Old New York*. Cornell University Press, 2020.

Niven, Penelope. *Steichen: A Biography*. Eastern National, 2004.

Peters, Margot. *Bernard Shaw and the Actresses: A Biography*. Garden City, New York: Doubleday & Company, 1980.

Peters, Margot. *Mrs. Pat: The Life of Mrs. Patrick Campbell*. New York: Alfred A. Knopf, 1984.

Preston, Diana. *Lusitania: An Epic Tragedy*. New York: Walker & Company, 2002.

Sanderson, Eric W. *Mannahatta: A Natural History of New York City*. Harry N. Abrams, Inc., 2009.

Scott, R. F. *Scott's Last Expedition*. Wordsworth Classics of World Literature, 2011.

Sheean, Vincent. *Oscar Hammerstein I: The Life and Exploits of an Impresario*. New York: Simon & Schuster, 1956.

Soucek, Gayle. *Mr. Selfridge in Chicago: Marshall Field's, the Windy City & the Making of a Merchant Prince*. The History Press, 2015.

Young, Louisa. *A Great Task of Happiness: The Life of Kathleen Scott*. Macmillan, 1995.

Mary Desti and son Preston from *The Untold Story: The Life of Isadora Duncan 1921-1927* by Mary Desti [1929].

Index

About the Author

Ken Zurski is a longtime broadcaster, author and speaker based out of Peoria, Illinois. A native of the Chicagoland area and a veteran of radio news, Ken released his first book, *The Wreck of the Columbia* in 2012. This is his fourth book and second in the *Unremembered* series. Ken resides in Morton, Illinois with his wife Connie, two children, Sam and Nora, and dog Molly.

Visit his website at unrememberedhistory.com, follow him on Facebook at @kenzurskiauthor or @unrememberedhistory, and find him on Twitter at @kzurski.

Made in the USA
Columbia, SC
09 September 2022